WILDERNESS AND

RAZOR WIRE

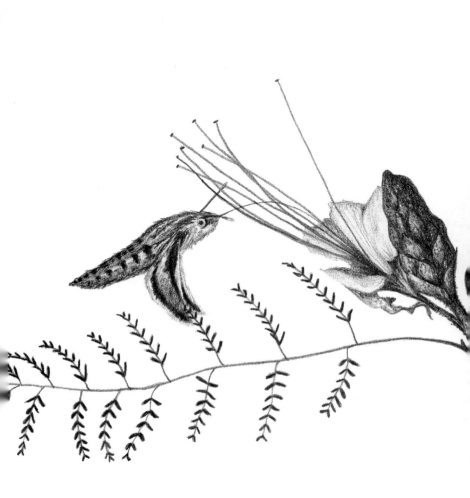

WILDERNESS AND

RAZOR WIRE

KEN LAMBERTON

WITH A FOREWORD BY
RICHARD SHELTON

MERCURY HOUSE
SAN FRANCISCO

Published in the United States by Mercury House, San Francisco, California, a nonprofit publishing company devoted to the free exchange of ideas and guided by a dedication to literary values. Visit us at www.wenet.net/~mercury.

United States Constitution, First Amendment: Congress shall make no law respecting an establishment of religion, or prohibiting the free exercise thereof; or abridging the freedom of speech, or of the press; or the right of the people peaceably to assemble, and to petition the Government for a redress of grievances.

Mercury House and colophon are registered trademarks of Mercury House, Incorporated.

All illustrations by Ken Lamberton. Cover illustration: "Mexican Paloverde." Title illustration: "Hawkmoth with Mexican Bird of Paradise." Author photograph page 219 by Karen Lamberton.

Editorial, design, and production work by Kirsten Janene-Nelson, Justin Edgar, Jeremy Bigalke, Steven Mockus, and Tamara Straus.

Printed on acid-free paper by Bang Printing, Brainerd, Minnesota.

This book is made possible thanks to generous support from the Lannan Foundation.

Library of Congress Cataloguing in Publication Data
Lamberton, Ken, 1958–
Wilderness and razor wire / Ken Lamberton ;
with a foreword by Richard Shelton.
p. cm.
ISBN 1-56279-116-8 (trade paperback)
1. Prisons—Arizona—Tucson. 2. Prisoners—Arizona—Tucson—
Biography. 3. Criminals—Rehabilitation—Arizona—Tucson. 4. Natural
history—Arizona—Tucson. 5. Santa Rita Prison (Tucson, Arizona). I. Title.
HV9481.T83L36 2000
508.791'77—DC21
99-33539
CIP

Even the sparrow has found a home,
And the swallow a nest for herself,
Where she may lay her young—

Psalm 84:3

CONTENTS

ACKNOWLEDGMENTS

The idea for *Wilderness and Razor Wire* came to me during the black, timeless days following my return to prison. It was only an idea, however, and would have remained so had it not been for so many people who have reached out to me in this place. My first thanks go to Patrick Lannan and Jeanie Kim of The Lannan Foundation, Los Angeles, for their generous support of this book and particularly the Creative Writing Workshop at Santa Rita and our magazine the *Walking Rain Review*, where my artwork and essays first found a home. Belief is contagious. To the workshop's director, Richard Shelton, I owe the soul of this book. You knew before I did that I had a story to tell, and your inspiration and insight gave me invaluable guidance in telling it. You are both mentor and friend. And, I am especially grateful for Lois Shelton, without whose diligence at the word processor through multiple rewrites this text would still be crude ink tracks on college-ruled paper.

I also wish to thank those editors and staff of literary journals who encouraged me to continue this project by publishing various chapters along the way: An early version of

"Stained Hands and Character Flaws" first appeared as "Desert's Child" in *Cimarron Review;* "Captive Species" was published in *Oasis;* "Raptors and Flycatchers" and "The Importance of Trees" in *Snowy Egret* (special thanks to Karl Barnebey, Philip Repp, Ruth Acker, et al., who honored me as Guest Editor of the Fall 1997 issue and nominated "Raptors and Flycatchers" for a Pushcart Prize); "Weeds" in *South Dakota Review;* "Wilderness and Razor Wire" (as "Wildtime") in *Northern Lights;* "Of Swallows and Doing Time" in *Manoa;* "The Wisdom of Toads" in *Puerto Del Sol;* "Raptors and Flycatchers" in *American Nature Writing 1999,* edited by John Murray; "Mesquite" in *Green Mountains Review;* "Queen" in *The Gettysburg Review;* "Weeds" in *Alligator Juniper;* and "Desert Time" in *you are here.* To my editors, Thomas Christensen and Kirsten Janene-Nelson, and all the staff at Mercury House, my appreciation for reading past the address on my proposal and for taking a chance with me, allowing me to share my wilderness.

Additionally, I'm indebted to fellow writers who patiently reviewed my manuscript in part or in whole and offered suggestions and encouragement. Many of you I only know through correspondence; all of you have become cherished friends: Marcia Bonta, Janice Bowers, Mary Beacom Bowers, Will Clipman, Alison Deming, Deidre Elliot, Gregory McNamee, Susan Tweit, Terry Tempest Williams, Ann Zwinger. Thanks for welcoming me into your community and even sharing an editor or agent. Your words are a part of me.

For the many ways I have been assisted in seeing past the razor wire I owe a great debt to my counselors and therapists, Dr. Paul Hanson, John Cepin, and Dr. Jennifer Schneider. To Albert Benz and Steve Gladish, I acknowledge your kindness to me, as you show to all of the men you work with and teach in prison. You concerned yourselves more with what I was going to do rather than with what I had done. And for the immeasurable gift of eighteen months' freedom with my family, my attorneys, Steve Sherick and Brian Rademacher of the Sherick Law Office, have my greatest respect and gratitude.

To family and friends who gave of your time, reading my essays, sending cards and letters, supporting me with sheets of stamps, you've stood by me as though in prison with me. Your names are too numerous to list, but I want to especially thank Brian Barnes, Eunice Burton, Tom Dinkins, Ernie Gomez, Debra Jones, Betty Ann Shelton, Coe and Marty Slattery, Jeff Teich. And finally I must thank my daughters, Jessica, Kasondra, and Melissa, for their unconditional enthusiasm in things wild and captive, and my wife, Karen, who insists that I never dedicate a book about prison to her and who faithfully questions every word I write, particularly those concerning hormones.

Ken Lamberton #61728

Working with prison inmates tends to channel one's thinking in extremely specific ways. There is "crime" and there is "punishment." We seldom stop to consider that many people commit crimes who are never punished, or that the extent and nature of the punishment often has no relation to the seriousness of the crime. It is a simplistic mind-set, but it is one all of us fall back on at times when faced with the incredible human complexity inside any American prison.

Another channel of thinking that structures the outlook of some who work with prisoners can be expressed in the traditional Christian terms of "guilt" and "innocence," "good" and "evil." This would be a simple perspective if it were not complicated by the equally demanding concepts of "forgiveness" and "mercy," also important elements in the Christian ethic.

Then there is the sociological view. It can, when highly simplified, come perilously close to being mechanistic, a matter of cause and effect. When I recently asked a group of inmates in my writing workshop to list what they considered to be the major factors that had led them into prison, they listed mostly sociological ones: childhood poverty, abusive parents, an inadequate education, alcoholism, the ready availability of drugs, etc. After we had discussed the lists, I suggested there might be one more basic reason that had not been mentioned. I was fishing, of course, and while they tried hard, only one person was able to come up with the answer. The inmate who got the right answer was Ken Lamberton. The answer was "stupidity."

I think all three of these schemas in viewing prison inmates have some legitimacy, although I fear any one of them when relied upon to the exclusion of all else. There is also a fourth perspective, but it would be applicable in so few cases that I can understand why it is seldom called into play, and probably only some old pedant like me would take it seriously. But in the case of Ken Lamberton, his crime, his family, and his present situation, I do take it seriously. If I step back for a moment and try to imagine Ken Lamberton's life as if he were a character on the stage, it all becomes immediately clear. His life is the modern version of an Aristotelian tragedy, and it fits Aristotle's pattern in all the basic essentials as much, I suspect, as could be possible in modern times.

Aristotle did not use the word *tragedy* as we do. We have a tendency to use the word in a casual way to refer to any misfortune, great or small. Aristotle said that tragedy was a sudden, dramatic fall from a high position (that is, it could occur only to a highly placed person), that it was often the result of a character flaw, and that it was the culmination of a series of events brought on by both the tragic hero (Aristotle didn't talk about heroines but he clearly included them) and the circumstances surrounding that hero, that is, the culture. It was, in short, the last step in a series of faulty steps on the part of a person of exemplary character who had somehow, perhaps because of a character flaw, taken the wrong path. Usually, when the tragic hero fell, as Macbeth or Othello fell, he took a great many others with him.

I have been teaching a workshop in the Arizona State Prison system since 1974, and of the hundreds of inmates I have gotten to know over the years, I can think of perhaps four men to whom this definition might possibly apply. But it applies most closely to Ken Lamberton, and it is curious that of all four of these young men, Ken is the only one whose fall did not involve violence. All of the others committed murder, either "crimes of passion" or rage while under the influence of drugs. Ken's crime was love—disastrous, misplaced, and foolish—but love nonetheless. He and his lover were as star-crossed as Romeo and Juliet, and equally mad, in the sense of madly in love. The big difference was that she was a fourteen-year-old girl and he was twenty-seven, married, and the father of a growing family. Shakespeare never utilized this plot because in his day the liaison would not have been illegal, no crime would have been committed.

To meet Ken, one would certainly not think of the tragic hero. He is quiet, diffident, a little lanky, nice looking, with closely cropped dark curly hair. If anything is striking about him now, I suppose it is his reserve, but I think some of that comes from his ten long years in prison and the caution that has come from being often in terrible danger. He speaks softly, laughs quietly, smiles and nods, but seldom says much. In the presence of his wife and children he is more animated, less on his guard. During his year of freedom, he was a student in my classes at the University of Arizona. He is the kind of graduate student who seldom speaks during a discussion

in class, but when he does, he has something important and
pertinent to say, and everyone listens. He has a quick intelli-
gence, grasping concepts with the same alertness with which
he recognizes a hawk. Yet there is a kind of innocence about
him, something hard to put one's finger on. He is not worldly-
wise. In fact, he is not worldly at all. His lack of bitterness in
light of all that has happened to him is remarkable. I am used
to working with men who complain loudly about their bad
treatment, as I most certainly would. After being attacked,
having his ear nearly severed and suffering broken ribs, Ken
shrugs, says, "It's over. I survived. Thank God for Karen who
got me transferred to a safer place."

For me, Ken's life fits the pattern of a modern Aristotelian tragedy in so many ways it is uncanny. He was highly
placed: well educated, very successful in all his activities,
chosen Science Teacher of the Year, beautiful wife and children. He may have had a tragic flaw. His wife suggests it
when she says he didn't know his limits. He was successful
at everything he tried. His fall seems to have been the result
of a series of events to which he succumbed because of some
inner lack or weakness. And lastly, when he fell, he took his
world (his family) with him, leaving them to face poverty
and humiliation.

We often read about crimes in terms of a perpetrator and
a victim, but nearly every crime has several victims. Often the
perpetrator of a crime is ultimately a victim of that crime and
suffers as much or more than the original victim. And the
families of those who commit crimes sometimes suffer more
than either the victim or the perpetrator. In this case, Ken's
entire family went down with him, but it went down with
enormous pride and dignity, largely because of Karen, the re-

markable woman who is his wife. And because of Karen's iron determination, it has risen again.

Many husbands have strayed as flagrantly as Karen's did, but because they strayed within the bounds of generally acceptable although frowned-on behavior, their wives were not exposed to public humiliation on a large scale. Karen was exposed to that humiliation, and she also had a husband returned to her by the police in a state of near-catatonia after the young woman for whom he had thrown it all away was taken, unwillingly, from him. Karen experienced all that any wife would experience when supplanted by a younger woman, and in addition there was the police, the media, the shock and shame, and how to tell the children what had happened. She knew that her husband's life and sanity, as well as the future of her family, depended on what she did. She was a genuinely religious young woman who loved her husband, and as she told me once, "Divorce is not an option in our family."

To say that Karen is willowy would be an understatement. She is so thin a stiff breeze could blow her away, and I think there is a family story about the time it did. "Family" is the definitive word here: Karen's strong, deeply religious parents, and her own and Ken's feeling for their family, their three daughters. Looking at this family from the outside, one would shudder to think about Ken's situation, given the nature of his crime and his formidable father-in-law, who could easily portray Moses or one of the Old Testament prophets. But somehow, it has worked out. That's a tribute to everybody involved. Ken and his father-in-law seem genuinely fond of one another. The family holds together. Friends rally around.

Of them all, I think that Karen has changed the most because of the extraordinary pressures placed upon her. She has gone to school, obtained degrees, worked as a paralegal, and mounted legal action that actually extricated her husband from prison for a year, although the action of a lower court was eventually overturned by a higher court and he was returned.

Karen has lifted herself and her children off welfare while battling, sometimes daily, to keep her husband safe and alive in a prison system that has often seemed bent upon placing him in situations where his status as "sex offender" would be a sure ticket to assault and possibly death.

All of this is information peripheral to Ken's book, and certainly not necessary to an understanding or appreciation of it. There is nothing sensational in his book, nothing to satisfy those who lick their lips at the mention of prison and all its dark, dirty secrets. But it is obvious from the book how Ken is managing to survive in prison and how, if he continues to survive, he will come out strong and focused on his life's work, observing and writing about the nature around him. He will not be able to return to the classroom—he knows that—but he will continue to teach through his writing, his insights into the natural world, and his quite remarkable drawings of the flora and fauna of that world, and he will teach a far larger number of people than he did in the classroom. He also knows that much of the incredible severity of his sentence—twelve years—resulted from the fact that he was a teacher, and that he violated a position of trust with one of his students.

Ken's book is the only work of its kind I know of, the point at which prison and the world of nature intersect, the moving point of the still world. He sees the natural world so intensely because at any minute he might be locked up in a cell, and he may never see it again. He writes quietly, matter-of-factly, but beneath his quiet tone is a desperation, a reaching up toward the swallows as they fly in and out of the prison yard. This book will become a quiet classic, another testimony to the grandeur of the human spirit under fire, the human spirit that can, in spite of mistakes so severe they shatter lives, rise again and fly with the swallows.

Richard Shelton
University of Arizona

Wilderness and

Razor Wire

Arizona Thistle

STAINED HANDS AND CHARACTER FLAWS

> Destiny marks you early in the day
> With a knowing finger,
> Then busies itself setting up the props,
> Painting the scenery.
> —Charles Simic, *Walking the Black Cat*

From this upper bunk where I write, a narrow window allows me a southern exposure of the desert outside my cell. An expanse of razed ground, marked with an artificial horizon of galvanized steel webbing, fills the lower two-thirds of the frame. But beyond the fence, an entire basin of creosote, mesquite, and cholla leans up against the hunched shoulders of the Santa Rita Mountains at the Mexican border. This evening, coyotes call to me with borderless voices from the desert's fringe, complaining about their vagrant allotment in life. I would gladly trade places with them.

My wilderness is a limited geographical area, not one bound by mountains or rivers or oceans, but by chain link and razor wire. My wilderness is a prison. All the same, it is a wilderness with its own nuances of seasonal change, summer droughts and winter freezes, rain, dust, and wind; with its own microcosm of weeds, trees, birds, and insects. Nature is here as much as it is in any national park or forest or monument, those places we always list whenever we speak of wilderness. Nature writer Alison Deming says that as a culture we need to outgrow the childish notion that nature takes place only in wilderness. Perhaps this is why some people hardly notice nature here. It would be a simple matter to wake up each morning as a body on a mattress that moves through another pointless day, a body at work raking rocks, a body at meals, a body in front of the TV, a body that would, undoubtedly, live without participating in life. It's easy to lack emotion, perception. What's difficult—but infinitely more rewarding—is to sense wilderness, to feel its moods, hear its migrations, see its shiftings and pulses. What's difficult is to have a sense of place ... in this place.

⊱┈✦┈○┈✦┈⊰

When I first came to this desert at the age of ten, I killed things. Whether spined, scaled, feathered, or furred, they all fell to my Wristrocket slingshot and Daisey pump BB gun. In the desert lot behind my house I hunted whiptail lizards to near-extirpation, hanging their broken bodies on the spines of a prickly pear cactus as if they were trophies of my budding manhood. Around my neighborhood I stalked songbirds to skin and mount following the directions of a mailorder taxidermy kit. I imagined I was James Ohio Pattie, Daniel Boone of the Southwest, using my skills as a trapper and explorer to survive off the land. But in truth the animals I killed were sacrifices offered up to my own selfish curiosity and ignorance. It had nothing to do with survival. Killing was my way of dealing with an environment I didn't understand, a brutal, arrogant reaction to its incomprehensible and awful strangeness. And because everything was strange, I killed over and over again. It was my first religion.

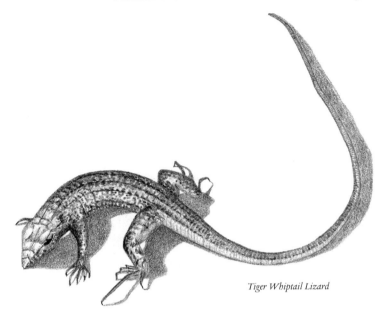

Tiger Whiptail Lizard

I paid particular attention to saguaros. At first I did this by using them for targets when throwing rocks, launching spears, or practicing with an archery set. Once, while trundling boulders in Pima Canyon, the collision between the opposing energies (kinetic versus potential) of a falling rock and stationary saguaro snapped four feet off the cactus's crown. The break was clean and sharp and exposed a circlet of skeleton wrapped in white, spongy flesh. It reminded me of a zucchini chopped in two. When I took to probing another saguaro with a sharpened stick, someone taught me another way to pay attention to saguaros.

"*What* are you doing there?" the man behind me asked. I tried to hide my sap-bloodied weapon, and turned to face my punishment. He had trapped me in his yard. To my surprise, however, he wasn't interested in scolding me and sending me home with burning ears. Instead, he diagrammed a cactus in

the dirt (with my stick) and explained the damage I was causing, damage like introducing bacteria into the wounds I had
made. It was a good lecture, but it would be a while before I
stopped persecuting saguaros.

As I got older I began visiting the front range of the
Santa Catalina Mountains: Pusch Ridge, Pima Canyon, Finger Rock, Sabino Canyon. Hiking here was intimate and ab-
sorbing. I learned the well-traveled trails and then avoided
them, choosing instead to bushwhack over bajadas and along
drainages and scale cliff faces. Each time I returned I became
more attuned to the inconspicuous—the furtive call of a
mourning dove in 110 degree heat, the pulse of water con-
stricted by rock. I learned that cicadas, cold-blooded insects,
love the heat. Their electric whine heralds the approach of
summer. I often came across the discarded skins of their larvae shortly after emergence, the keratinous casings clinging
to branches and twigs of mesquite trees like split seedpods.
For a few short weeks the male's monotonous serenade
called females to breed, completing an annual cycle. I loved
them for their constancy; they cued me to the rhythms of the
desert. Even now I hear their seasonal chorus in my mind;
my ears fairly ring with it. For me, it is an epiphany, not unlike the advent of the summer monsoons.

Returning to the Catalinas again and again always brought
new experiences. The familiar defiles and outcrops, the canyons and ridges and peaks offered deeper layers of detail with
each trip. I wasn't satisfied only to make an acquaintance with
the landscape. I desired romance. Even more, I
wanted the kind of relationship where romantic chance encounters would be the inter-
locking strands of some new and profound
ecological vision, where I wasn't a mere

Apache Cicada

observer but a participant, where I was connected and my place made sense.

Not surprisingly, the killing didn't stop. But the killing —actually, I preferred the term "collecting"—did become less meaningless. There was a kind of intimacy with the act. Body parts became my personal tutors. A four foot pelican wing modeled flight mechanics; a tray of skulls illustrated eating habits. I noticed how the imbricated scales of reptiles matched the same pattern in the feathers of birds. I started keeping more dead things in the freezer. My dresser drawers doubled as museum drawers, socks making room for the skin tubes of snakes and birds; underwear for mammal hides.

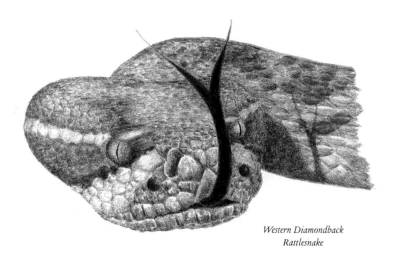

Western Diamondback
Rattlesnake

When friends discovered my taxidermy hobby, they brought me gifts of roadkills, deceased pets, victims of pool drownings. My driver's license was my salvage permit. No still shape in the road got past my scrutiny; I was always looking for new species. I grew fond of certain stretches of road, particularly on night drives, expecting additional specimens for my collections, sometimes making those specimens myself, by running them down.

I collected pets, too. I set up aquariums for fish and aquatic insects taken from local creeks, for marine invertebrates smuggled across the border from the Gulf of California. I built terrariums for toads and cages for protected Gila monsters and rattlesnakes. I hatched Gambel's quail in a homemade incubator and trained red-tailed and Harris' hawks for hunting. Throughout my high school and early college years my bedroom was a hissing, squawking, bubbling menagerie. I wanted two of every kind but, unlike Noah, the only freedom I ever gave my animals came by way of their death. I had no conservation ethics, a serious flaw in my desired ecological vision. The desert had opened up to me and taught me about its intricacies, its relationships and dependencies. But what I didn't know, possibly because I had chosen to ignore it, was that I was out of balance. There wasn't any purpose in my desert education. I was taking, and giving nothing back.

I went to college to study biology, unavoidably, it seems. This formal education attempted to redefine my background experiences with nature, labeling them and tying them up into neat packages like cuts of beef. But it seemed necessary at the time, this idea of a concrete foundation in science. I benefited from upper-level courses like invertebrate zoology and marine biology. But my favorite classes lacked textbooks altogether. In one class, "Selective Studies in Malacology," the professors outnumbered the students. We spent a week together in the mountains of northern Mexico searching for snails. I returned with a tiny boojum tree that I had shoveled from the ground at Punta Cirio, the only place the rare succulent grows on mainland Mexico. Border officials quarantined the boojum, but a fat chuckwalla, hidden under my shirt, escaped detection. This course offered more than knowledge and experience. It offered specimens for my collections, new species to catalogue and file away.

I married in my senior year. Karen, born and raised in the desert, was the perfect partner for me. She was the assistant curator of my collections, accompanying me to the beaches of Mexico and the mountains of the Southwest. She also had taken lessons in the Catalinas. As we moved from homes to dorm rooms to apartments, she learned to care for fish tanks and birds of prey, and chuckwallas. It wasn't until I finally graduated and settled into teaching that my collections found a purpose outside my own pleasure. Now, everything, my entire life's experiences and all its natural extensions—hobbies, interests, and talents—came to focus on teaching biology. It seemed my life was making sense.

Within a few years of teaching (supported, as always, by my wife) I had branched out away from the classroom and into extracurricular programs that included a science club, which traveled throughout the state on monthly wilderness expeditions, an after-school taxidermy class, and an annual wild food cooking and eating event we dubbed "The Beast Feast." These were wonderful tangents from a classroom structure of books, lectures, and notes. My students became the center of learning and I took a seat next to them, scribbling notes instead of regurgitating facts. We relied on what I called "teachable moments," gifts from the desert that came by chance, serendipity. Lesson plans here were sacrilege. On an expedition we might have found a tarantula out prowling for a mate after a storm, or we might have gotten a soaking. Both could have been lessons. My collections, caged and displayed in my classroom, weren't just curious spectacles with sounds and smells; they were the subjects of discussions, planned and impromptu. Now my students would often bring me gifts, both alive and dead—so many, in fact, that I didn't have space for them all. Of course, I couldn't get rid of anything. Some, like the turtles, I let roam in my room.

Because teaching took Karen and me to another city away from Tucson, our hometown, we traveled a lot the first years. One strip of road along Highway 89, the Pioneer Parkway, was our favorite. The parkway, a botanical reserve with rest stops, monuments, and picnic areas, was less con-

Regal Horned Lizard

gested and more interesting than the freeways. It was also a grocery store for road kills.

Training hawks for falconry demanded quantities of fresh meat, preferably with the roughage intact (skin, bone, fur, feathers). Not only did the parkway provide this road kill cuisine, but it also produced the salvage for my taxidermy students. On the parkway great horned owls were accustomed to preying on rodents as they skittered across the warm pavement, their cheek pouches stuffed with the seeds of grasses that thrived on the road's margins. Unfortunately, the owl's habits for easy pickings periodically cost them their lives. One night, I found two of them, lying like feather pillows in the road, their bodies warm and eyes bright as though only resting. Whereas other animals usually melded with the asphalt, their broken forms like divots of turf, heavy with death, the owls seemed as though they might take flight at any moment. Driving home with them on the floor of my cab, I wondered what I'd do if one suddenly rose up in life, huge talons slashing at me for freedom.

It was this apparent vitality, even limp in death, that made great horned owls such appealing subjects for taxidermy. When a local newspaper ran a feature story about my taxidermy class, my students offered interviews while giving the reporter and his photographer quite a performance, scraping hides, shampooing birds, touching up head mounts. The article appeared as a full page spread in the lifestyle section. The publicity pleased the school, but I had one concern. The reporter had failed to mention any permit to preserve wildlife for educational purposes. I didn't have any permit, only a letter from the Game and Fish.

I was in the middle of teaching third period Life Science when two uniformed wildlife officers walked into my room. They were serious. I left my class and followed them to the teachers' area. "We need to see your animals and your permit," the man in the U.S. Fish and Wildlife uniform said. "Okay," I answered. I directed them to my lab area, dug out some paperwork, and opened the freezer. The Fish and Wildlife officer was not happy with my paperwork. "You should have a federal salvage permit," he told me. "You're in possession of federally protected animals." Fortunately, my letter was enough to disappoint them. I would get a lecture but no citations. After they were gone the principal of the school told me how they had charged into her office, threatening to arrest me. The whole incident unnerved me, but it was the "saguaro lecture" all over again. My behavior didn't change.

I wish I could say now this encounter with the law made some difference. I can't, however. Within a few months I got caught cleaning quail shot out of season. Some people saw me cleaning the birds, some of which were ripe with eggs. The gravid quail interested me. They became a dissection, a lesson. But the spectators were not pleased and objected to what for me was just another "teachable moment." When I got home, a game warden was waiting for me. The citation cost me a hundred dollars and my reputation as a sportsman. Maybe it was an indication of a character flaw, this business of killing and blood. It certainly was an indication of a disregard for game laws, much less any conservation ethics. On a previous occasion a police officer stopped me after an evening of dove hunting. He noticed that blood had soaked my hands and asked if I had been injured. "No," I said. I couldn't tell him that I had a foolish macho tradition of showing off my unwashed hands following a hunt; that, tonight, after cleaning my kill, I had bought a cherry Coke at a Circle K, blood and feathers sticking to my hands. The officer's concern should have embarrassed me. Instead, I was afraid of getting a fine for possessing twice the legal limit of doves. Fortunately, the officer must have thought I was only sadistic and not necessarily a criminal. He checked my hunting license—not bothering to count the birds—and told me to get my tail lights fixed.

Maybe I was sadistic. Blood held a measure of fascination for me. My wife thought it was juvenile, but I wasn't sure she understood. She had had enough of blood. To her, blood meant weakness and loss and pain: the blood of menstruation, of irretrievable innocence, of childbirth. Blood was a source of shame and disgust, something personal and private; when confronted with it she always washed her hands. But to me, the pride of life was blood; it was a sign of strength. Blood on my hands, extraneous blood, meant that I was a survivor, that I was in control of my world.

Inevitably, this bloodlust of mine wouldn't surrender.

The desert had been trying to lead me, little by little, away from this antiquated concept of manhood, but I was stubborn, childish. I was a child of the desert, nursed, weaned, and raised with heat and thirst, thorn, and wound, but I never matured. My intimacy with living things came from killing them. It was a character flaw. Wilderness convert Aldo Leopold, says, "Man always kills the thing he loves ..." I killed what loved me.

Worse, my flaw reached beyond my relationship with the desert to other relationships. In the year of my greatest success as a teacher, I dishonored the whole profession by becoming romantically, and sexually, involved with one of my former students. At a time when my wife, only five years into our marriage and pregnant with our third child, had become my closest, most precious companion, I struck at the very core of her womanhood. I humiliated her publicly, then abandoned her and our children. I was no different from that selfish child at ten. I tried to destroy all that was good in my life.

⊶⊷⊶O⊷⊶⊷

On some evenings, when the sun angles its rays just right, I can see from my cell window the coyotes outside the fence. They are ghosts, appearing only as they move, zigzagging, noses to the ground, disappearing again when something catches their attention. In this way, they slip along the boundaries in my life, always in the shadows, wary, elusive. There are many coyotes out there. More than I know. They represent only a fraction of the wilderness I've encountered here, much of which, by wind or wing or some other means, even crosses the boundaries and leaks into this place. I choose to look beyond the fences, or among them, for the wilderness, the mountains, the desert, the coyotes. I choose to look

Coyote

for something "with the residue of God" as Rick Bass says, rather than something with the residue of man.

Aside from an occasional insect, I no longer kill things. I haven't bloodied my hands in ten years. It's a shame, tragedy really, that I had to come to prison to find inside me the ability to move closer, at least somewhat, to an ecological awareness, a sense of earth and sky, to see the importance of unselfish relationships, my marriage and family, and to participate in life. Karen and my daughters aren't allowing me to start over. Even the desert doesn't give you a second chance. What they (and the desert) *have* offered me may be more painful than a new beginning: a way to continue, a way to give something back.

My first evening back at Santa Rita.

I wash laundry to take the "fish" out of my denim jeans. The new pants are not only oversized, stiff, and uncomfortable, but they betray me as the recent arrival I am. I've done nearly eight years on this prison yard. I don't want to look inexperienced, vulnerable, scared. It will take several washings to get the look out of my clothes; getting it off my face is another matter.

Outside the laundry room, a lone Mexican bird of paradise dominates a dirt rectangle between a concrete pad and brick wall. The lanky plant blooms despite neglect, despite the cigarette butts and gray flags of lint that fertilize the hardpan. Among brackenlike leaves, yellow flowers let loose their stamens as if they were butterflies unfurling multitudes of long, red tongues. Beneath whole cones of flowers, bean pods stand erect and fat on their stems, some dried to the edge of bursting, others already rolled into seed-flung paper straws.

I'm recalling the sound of exploding seedpods on heat-quieted summer afternoons when a hawkmoth arrives on blurred wings. My ears thrum. Its agile, darting movements immobilize me; my limbs feel awkward, heavy, as they do whenever I see those television commercials of Grecian models demonstrating NordicTrac, and I'm shamefully aware of my presence. I'm a blundering example of Pleistocene megafauna by comparison. But I notice something else too. A bit of wildness enters me, like a slight gust of wind fills a sail. It is an unmeasurable thing, this wildness, and though I cannot touch it, I feel fortunate for its connection with me.

Tongue to tongue, the hawkmoth completes the bird of paradise. Together, the two are the most natural pair in the world, and I will never see the flowers again without thinking "hawkmoth." Books tell me this insect, the white-lined sphinx moth, is an important pollinator of desert plants, visiting the nocturnal blooms of sacred datura, Ajo lily, and evening primrose. Its enormous tongue allows it to dip into the deep wells of rare cactus blossoms also, like those of the night-blooming cereus. What's most striking to me is the insect's uninsectlike traits. It has hummingbird qualities, not just in its size and rapid wingbeats and backward flight, but down in its cells. "Insect" here seems a fluid concept. The moth flies across the boundaries of what's insect and what's bird. It's hot-blooded; shivering its flight muscles on cool days to raise its body above ambient temperature. A hairy furze coats its length and guards against heat loss in the same way that feathers insulate birds. *Hawk*moth may be a misnomer. *Hummingbird*moth captures the insect's essence.

Overhead, as if defying the impossible distances between birds and stars, nighthawks glide on tapered wings through the Summer Triangle, finding the effort of wingbeat unnecessary. But I am in the company of a hawkmoth. The hummingbird mimic christens the evening of my return.

Hawkmoth

Barn Swallow

OF SWALLOWS AND DOING TIME

The wind always blows here. It gathers itself into a steady pulse from the south and breaks across the prison yard with its load of blond talcum. I'd forgotten about the wind. I've been back only a day and already it greets me with its forlorn touch. The feeling wants to overwhelm me. The barn swallows welcome me too, the graceful birds darting here and there in the wind like dark hands throwing gang signs. They know how to take advantage of the wind. But do they know how to deal with the loneliness, the melancholy, the time?

Had anyone said I'd see this place again after gaining my freedom in December 1994, I wouldn't have believed him. My release was a miracle in itself, and now, it seems, it's a miracle I'm back. Eighteen months after a superior court judge ordered me home to my wife and three daughters, the appellate court overturned his decision, returning me to prison to finish the outstanding four years of my twelve-year sentence. Serving nearly eight years wasn't enough to satisfy the appellate court judges concerning my crime. Not that I can complain; I am guilty.

In 1986, I was named Teacher of the Year for Mesa Public Schools. Five years of teaching and already I was in my niche and finding success. I believed I was invulnerable. Then, at the end of that school year, as I mentioned previously, I became infatuated with one of my students. Infatuation led to romance and then obsession. We ran away together to start a new life in Colorado. After a two-week affair in Aspen, someone from Mesa recognized us and notified the police. They arrested me while we walked hand-in-hand along the plaza. The girl went back to school, and I went to prison. I was twenty-seven years old; she was fourteen.

The miracle was not so much that my wife Karen could get me out of prison in the first place … but that she would want to. I had deserted her, degraded her with a long list of abuses—the stigma of being a convict's wife on welfare relatively minor in comparison to being the wife of a nationally publicized sex offender—and yet she set aside her humiliation and shifted from housewife to law student. Six years after my arrest, raising three girls on her own, she had earned a paralegal degree and a political science degree, and had begun working for a criminal law firm in Tucson. It was her work on my case that got her hired and, with the assistance of two sympathetic (unpaid) lawyers, that won my release.

Now I'm back, and it feels as if I've been arrested and convicted all over again. Unlike the swallows, which migrate in and out of this place, my cycle of freedom has left me defenseless, insecure, disoriented. Four more years. The time weighs heavily on me.

I find Brad in an empty classroom where he is waiting for his next student. He teaches the men, mostly Mexican nationals, how to read and write; English literacy is a requirement in the Arizona correctional system regardless of where you're from. I haven't seen Brad for two summers, and he's pleased to tell me about his barn swallow observations during my absence. Brad is dying. Has been dying for twenty years, but he's getting closer now. He's in his seventies and can't squeeze much more time out of this place, already outlasting cancer in his bowels, a colostomy, and its necessary bag that his blue T-shirt could never hide.

Brad's moleskin face splits open and his eyes unglaze when he talks about the birds. He's been watching a nest on the run near his cell since the swallows daubed the mud-pellet cup to the block wall four summers ago. "Three successful nests this time!" he says, exposing several gray and black-rooted teeth. The dentist will pull those soon, I think. "First time ever they've raised three broods in one summer," he continues and laughs. There's swallow-pleasure in his eyes, and I believe for a moment that the birds allow him to forget about this place, his dying. Like the man in my creative writing workshop who also watches the swallows, and writes about them in haiku. If the guards even suspected that there are men here who escape on those dark, narrow wings, if only for a short time in their minds, they'd shoot the birds.

><>–O–<><

"There are those birds you gauge your life by," says Terry Tempest Williams. "Each year, they alert me to the regularities of the land." For her, those birds are burrowing owls. For me, they are the barn swallows. I was here, in prison at the Santa Rita Unit, when the swallows arrived for the first time in the spring of 1990. Theirs was a tentative advent. Only three pairs came to breed under the visitation ramada, hauling thousands of beak-sized adobe bricks one at a time to construct their pueblo nests. I watched them with my wife and daughters as the dark crescents rolled from the sky to streak through the vaulted structure, each one spinning and weaving in an aerial dance as precise as if every movement had been choreographed and practiced a thousand times. We were familiar with the common birds on the yard, the greasy-black grackles and cowbirds, the beggar house sparrows. Even my three-year-old daughter Melissa could name them. But the swallows were different, Stealth Fighters by comparison. Our eyes were drawn to their sleek bodies with their metallic, blue-black sheen and pumpkin breasts, long tapering wings and deeply forked tails. Such poetry from a pointed, seven-inch frame. And voices to match: a cheerful, liquid twittering of notes on descending and ascending scales. That summer, the transients raised twelve offspring, and by the end of September they were gone, migrating south as the first Pacific cold fronts prodded the Southwest. I remember hoping they would return, wondering if their experiment in nesting here at Santa Rita had been successful enough to bring them back.

Meanwhile, I began to gather stuff on barn swallows. The prison library offered some information but it was general, encyclopedic. I wrote the Tucson Audubon Library and connected with a kind and helpful woman named Joan Tweit who sent me more material, never seeming concerned that she was corresponding with a criminal. (Joan proved an invaluable source for me over the years. I finally met her after my temporary release from prison at a book-signing for her daughter, Susan, a natural history writer.) My wife also became a tremendous resource by perusing the periodical stacks at the University of Arizona Science Library and photocopying research articles from professional journals like *The Auk* and *Condor.*

Soon, I was learning things about swallows. And, because of this knowledge, I started considering why they had suddenly come to Santa Rita in the first place. By the end of March the following year, as the mesquite and desert willow finally shrugged winter from their dark branches, I was watching for them every day. I worked as a teacher's aide in a classroom next to the visitation ramada and every birdlike movement outside the picture windows got my attention. During evening church services in the same classroom I waited for that quick flash of wings and sickle-like projectile, that phantom silhouette that could only mean *swallow.* Then one Friday in mid-April, as the sun flattened on the western horizon and the sky turned cayenne, something dipped under the ramada. I stared and a few seconds later saw it again. I was sure. They were back.

Over the next month the birds reclaimed two nests from the previous year and refurbished them, packing fresh muddy pellets onto the lip of the old nest cup and reinforcing the work with bits of dried grass. The third nest, also left over from last season, was in dispute. My family and I amused ourselves with the drama of two flustered swallows who couldn't drive out some obstinate squatters. A pair of house sparrows had built a grassy nest neatly on the top of their nest and wouldn't budge. I was convinced that bird vocabulary includes swear words; their arguments lasted two weeks before the swallows finally resigned to sticking a new nest onto some other joist. A month or so after their arrival three pairs of barn swallows were brooding clutches of four or five speckled white eggs. By the end of June another two had joined them. It was small, but it was a colony.

I had read that barn swallows often nest in large groups: as many as fifty-five nests have been found in a single barn. They also seem to prefer human-made structures—barns, bridges, boat docks—especially if they're near open fields, meadow, marshes, or ponds where insects are abundant. The birds are voracious bug-netters, one swallow scooping up hundreds in a day. At the prison, swallows will work a large field in the morning and evening, sailing low to the ground and weaving a block pattern, dipping to intercept their prey, usually lacewings, flies, and moths. In fact, it's these fields, I believe, that originally attracted barn swallows to Santa Rita. The fields and their insect complement.

In 1989, before swallows nested at Santa Rita, the Arizona Department of Corrections changed how it dealt with its wastewater at the Tucson complex. Prisons were getting crowded, tents had gone up, cells were being double-bunked. We were taxing the sewage treatment plant, and its settling ponds had begun to flow. The reclaimed water needed somewhere to go; we didn't have a golf course. So, what was once dust and creosote between the complex's main units (there were three of them at the time: Cimarron, Rincon, and Santa Rita) suddenly became an artificial wetland of weeds and grasses, kept verdant and soggy by a new effluent irrigation system. Twenty-one hundred men flushing toilets had turned the desert green.

I noticed the difference in bird life almost immediately. Ravens still probed the trash dumpsters while sparrows, starlings, and Brewer's blackbirds winnowed the dirt behind the dining areas for crumbs. Cowbirds still roved the soccer and softball fields en masse. But as the evening floodings fertilized the air and the new wetlands, I started counting mallards, gadwalls, killdeer, and great blue herons. When a flock of whimbrels flew over I was certain the birds were lost. Mourning doves by the hundreds, all coming from separate directions by twos and threes late in the afternoons, would congregate in the grass before flying off together to their roosts. My life list for birds seen in prison doubled, then tripled as I added western meadowlark, lark bunting, Say's phoebe, olivaceous and ash-throated flycatchers, western kingbird, yellow-headed blackbird, Cooper's hawk, and burrowing owl. And then once, for most of the morning, a great egret, all legs and beak, stationed itself in the center of the field. I'd never seen feathers so white; it was a blank cutout from a green page. When it wandered into an area of standing water I half expected it to spear a fish. As I write this now, I find I'm not surprised that the wetland and its insect forage created by the prison's water reclamation project drew the barn swallows. I'm sure they're more common in the desert than whimbrels and egrets.

For the ramada colony 1991 was not a good year at Santa Rita. Another breeding pair had constructed a fifth nest in August, but not a single chick had fledged. It was getting late; something was wrong. The only chicks I had seen were scrawny and naked. My daughters had found two under a nest on one of their visits. Both were dead. What confused me was the apparent contradiction of a solitary nest I had found about half a mile away at the Cimarron Unit. (I traveled there every Sunday for a creative writing workshop.) By August, two swallows at Cimarron had already raised six offspring and had started a second brood. Why was this solitary pair of swallows producing healthy birds while the ramada colony only dead chicks? I believed there were two keys that unlocked this riddle: the nature of bird colonies in general and the nature of our weather in particular. I didn't jump to this conclusion in a moment of inspiration; the idea come slowly. As I read the work of scientists who had studied barn swallows, one question kept surfacing: why colonies? It seemed, according to ample field observations, that the cost of nesting together should be too great, that competition for nesting areas, food, mates, and a higher likelihood that predators such as raccoons might discover and destroy a whole colony would conspire against colonial nesting. (The best argument I found *for* barn swallow colonies involved the bird's preference for nesting places already established in ideal habitats with a history of reproductive success. Talk about your chicken or the egg story!) Colonies just didn't seem like much of an advantage for barn swallows. On the other hand, solitary nesters had none of these problems. No competition for resources, less chance of predation.

I knew this, but it still didn't mean anything to me. It was the second key—the weather—that really helped me make sense out of the riddle. In southern Arizona the summer of 1991 turned out to be one of the driest in recent years. High temperatures averaged around 105 degrees. The monsoon storms were late, shrinking the normal amount of rainfall for that year by inches. One result of this unusual weather, and a serious problem for the brooding ramada colony, was a drought of flying insects. I had an idea that limited food resources, due to the failed monsoons, were working against the Santa Rita colony because there were too many birds in the area. The solitary barn swallows at Cimarron, however, because of less competition for food, were doing fine.

I sent a letter to Mary Beacom Bowers, then editor of *Bird Watcher's Digest,* telling her about my conclusions and suggesting that I write a feature about the barn swallows at Santa Rita. She had already published one article of mine about Harris' hawks, saying in her acceptance letter, "I get a lot of articles from prisoners, most of them invariably bad. Yours is different, however …" We were developing a good relationship and she definitely wanted to see my barn swallow piece. She published it in the March/April 1993 issue with a photograph of a single swallow gripping a strand of barbed wire. Quite appropriate, I thought, for an article from a writer "*based* in Arizona."

When I wrote about the barn swallows for *Bird Watcher's Digest* I didn't know where the ramada colony was headed. I continued writing notes about its progress, counting the number of nests and chicks, for the next four seasons until my release in 1994. The colony seemed to be just holding on. Now that I'm back I notice it is gone. Perhaps I had been right: the prison yard and its flex and flux of insects can't support it. I could blame the weather. I could also blame the visitation guards who began knocking down the nests (to keep the ramada free of the "mess" the birds made), thereby destroying the historical attractiveness of the site. Once I tried to explain to an officer the necessity of leaving the nests alone even after the birds were gone. He looked at me as if I were crazy and said nothing. I felt like a fool.

But even though the colony has dissolved, the birds still hang on. Solitary pairs have begun building nests under the eaves of the runs at some of the cell blocks, spreading them out so that there is only one, or at most two, nests on each of the four yards. Like the swallows at Cimarron, the birds have found an alternative to colony life. And now, out among the inmates, they're better for it.

Today, Steve brings me a swallow he's found injured and wants to know what he can do. I see one wing has a red bruise underneath it and tell him it may survive if he can get it to eat. Risking disciplinary action for an unlawful pet, he carries the tiny bird to his cell and makes a simple perch for it under his television. While the swallow sits quietly Steve stalks the run for flies, flyswatter in hand. He offers the freshest morsels to his charge but the bird ignores them. It refuses his nudges and proddings: Steve won't force it. Tonight, the swallow will slip from its perch and flutter mothlike on Steve's bunk. Steve won't know what to do except to hold it until the spasms stop, watching as one foot extends to grasp at nothing and then grasps no more.

The men whose cells happen to be near a swallow nest continue to impress me with their sensitivity for the birds. This was unexpected for me. I'm referring to men like Steve. Or Brad, who is fiercely protective of his swallow family, who monitors its growth year after year, counting eggs and chicks, marking off the days to hatching and fledgling, watching for additional broods. "I counted thirty this morning," he told me yesterday. "All of them singin' and carryin' on. I'm gonna miss 'em when they're gone." It's September, and I've noticed it too. The swallows are gathering in preparation for the migration south, and I'm wondering how I will have changed by the time they return … and if time will still have weight.

I realize that years ago the swallows had been allowing me to feel the weight of time and, in doing so, to feel the pain of remorse for what I had done. I had accepted this; the swallows have shown me the first steps toward change, toward health. Now, seeing them in this place again, a measure of hope returns. There's more than the heaviness of time.

It's ironic, thinking about it, how overcrowding in this prison and the solution to its consequent wastewater problem has affected the inmates here, has affected me. Twenty-one hundred men flushing their toilets has done more than settle the dust under a mat of vegetation. It's turned this bleak place into a wildlife island, a rest stop and refuge for wings and beaks and talons. And every spring, and for five or six months following, it's given us the swallows, gifts of grace on narrow wings.

I gauge my life by the swallows. Their nature, like many things in the world, is cyclic; they live inside the regular heartbeat of the land. Ebb and flow, flex and flux, rise and fall. It's a pattern I can live with, one that gives me hope. As long as the swallows come in the spring and go in the fall, come and go and come, I'll feel their rhythm, measuring it out as a change of seasons. This is the source of my hope: the swallows don't only make me feel the weight of time, they cue me to the passage of time. Where ancient peoples raised stones to track equinoxes and solstices, the swallows are my Stonehenge. In a place where clocks and calendars are meaningless, where hours and days and months percolate into one homogenous, stagnant pond, I mark the swallows.

Cooper's Hawk

As much as the migrations of swallows cue me to the passage of time, prison strives to keep me suspended in time, focused on, even obsessed with, the events that brought me here. It's not easy to go on with your life in this place. Prison isn't designed that way.

Eight PM. Lockdown. Outside it's dark, quiet. A guard walks the run, pulling on doors, peering into cells, making count. Face to I.D. count. I clip my yellow picture I.D. into the narrow window: ADC INMATE. THE BEARER OF THIS CARD IS UNDER THE CUSTODY AND JURISDICTION OF THE ARIZONA DE-PARTMENT OF CORRECTIONS. After she passes by my cell door, I brush my teeth, urinate, and climb into my bunk. My cell mate, wearing headphones (thankfully), watches "America's Most Wanted" on his TV, the screen's florescent images mirrored in his glasses.

This place could swallow me alive—a recurring thought I'm having lately. It's not only the physical confinement, but the emotional. How I feel is inconsequential; nothing gets beyond these walls. The mind-numbing routine, worthlessness, loneliness—how I feel about any of this stays locked inside me most of the time, unless I express it as inadequate words put down on paper. My worst fear is that I could lose what little I do have: the routine, a teaching job, my exercise walks, the privileges—phone calls, visits, the writing workshop. I could get transferred without notice to some impoverished corner of the state, cut off and forgotten, and then survive the experience for years. It happens. What's frightening is the lack of distraction, of contact with the world.

A distraction: I reread a letter from my daughter Kasondra. She writes that Raincloud (her sister Melissa's cat) is getting mail now. "He got a note from the vet. It's time for his shots." She says that I'm also getting mail, "but not for shots," she assures me.

Kasondra also tells me she's seen the Cooper's hawks again. "Remember when the mom hawk dive-bombed your head?" she asks. "Did that hurt?" I smile with the memory, combing my fingers through my hair, touching my scalp. A few months before the appellate court rescinded my freedom and ordered me back to prison, a pair of Cooper's hawks had nested in a large eucalyptus tree near my daughter's elementary school. At the time, I was writing an article for *Tucson Lifestyle* about a "raptor invasion" of our city—great horned owls, Harris' hawks, Cooper's hawks—and I'd been interested in this pair all spring. Whenever I drove past the school I checked on the birds. This time I got too close.

On the first day of summer vacation, Kasondra and I took a break from helping her fifth grade teacher clean out his classroom, an act of appreciation my wife likes to arrange with our daughters' teachers at the end of every school year. We crossed the parking lot holding hands and headed toward the tree. She was nervous. She knew several classmates whom the hawks had "dive-bombed" for approaching their nest.

"Don't worry," I said. "The hawks might swoop at us, but they won't hurt us. They'll try to warn us away."

Falconry had taught me about hawks. Karen and I had trained redtails and Harris' hawks during the first years of our marriage. It was something I had carried into our relationship that Karen enjoyed doing with me. (She often joked that keeping a hawk demanded as much attention as caring for a baby—without the convenience of diapers.) The behavior of Cooper's hawks was not unfamiliar to me. I knew what to expect.

We walked around the eucalyptus until I found a window through the branches where the nest was visible. It was an irregular mass of dark sticks high on the main trunk of the tree. Both parents stood over it, and beneath them, in the shade of their drooping wings, two white chicks panted in the heat.

"Can you see them?" I asked Kasondra.

"Yeah. I see two babies and the mom and dad."

Just then, the larger female flew off into another tree and began complaining in a high-pitched *kek, kek, kek, kek, kek.* Kasondra gripped my hand. "We better go, Dad."

"It's all right. She definitely doesn't want us around."

Kasondra moved close to me and hung on my arm as the female Cooper's flew over our heads, keening the whole distance, and perched behind us on a power pole.

She was crouched, facing us, calling in agitation. I recognized the stance of a hunting bird. "Okay, you're right," I said. "We should go." I turned my back to the hawk and we began walking away.

Kasondra never took her eyes off the bird. Suddenly, she squeezed my arm and said, "Dad!"

I felt a terrific blow on the back of my head. I stumbled

forward, my eyes burning. "Ouch!" I yelled and grabbed my head. "Man, that hurt!"

"I told you," Kasondra said as we ran back to her classroom.

Now, reading her letter again, she wants to know if I remember. How could I forget? I was bleeding when we got to her classroom. My wife counted five puncture wounds. She cleaned them, one by one, in front of Kasondra's teacher as my chastisement.

"At least she did not hit so hard that it knocked you down," Kasondra writes.

I put the letter away and snap off my reading lamp. I stare through the darkness, the concrete walls, the distance and time, and see the images her words have recalled for me, reflections in my mind. Nights are the worst here. If I were home now, I might play my guitar and sing Sixties' folk tunes to my daughters for bedtime. *Scarborough Fair, Pass it On, One Tin Soldier* are their favorites. Afterward, I might hunt for their kittens. Raincloud for Melissa. Mittens for Kasondra. Lucky for Jessica. Live animals held tightly among the stuffed ones. Then, after glasses of water, we might say our prayers. I should be home with them. Instead, alone, I read their letters, think about them, pray for them, and regret all that I'm missing in their lives and can never regain.

My wife—and others—would tell me I should have thought about this before I committed the crime. Everybody has 20/20 hindsight. The statement is so true it's a cliché. But, like other trite admonitions, it strikes me as shallow. Maybe all I want is sympathy. Of course I should've thought about it, but I didn't, couldn't. I could never have imagined the full consequences of my behavior at the time, and, even if I had, I'm not sure it would've mattered. Such is the nature of so-called "crimes of passion." I wasn't thinking. I was reacting to the opiates of feelings without considering what might happen in the future. And, in my foolishness, these powerful emotions made it right. Now, I know better, but it makes no difference. I have to eat the fruit of my misplaced passion of ten years ago. So does my family. For me, emotions unchecked are like excessive drinking or drug abuse. They can be devastating. Telling me I should have thought about this before I committed the crime is like telling a man lying in the gutter he should have thought about the likelihood of losing everything when he took his first sip of alcohol. He would only agree with you from the gutter, where the advice is too late.

I don't need anyone to tell me what I should have been thinking when. This place keeps it fresh in my mind. The walls and fences, dehumanizing guards, the fear and depression and guilt, rub my face in the events of that summer.

In June of 1986, with my teaching responsibilities finished for the year, we moved to our residence at a youth camp in the northern foothills of the Santa Catalina Mountains where we had met eight seasons earlier. The ranch camp wasn't only a job for us; it was a second home. In 1981, eighteen months after that first meeting, Karen and I exchanged vows in the camp's outdoor chapel. Two summers later, Jessica arrived, conveniently on our day off. Then came Kasondra during Christmas camp. Our lives, our growing family—there was a belief that camp water not only caused pregnancy but girls as well—were entwined with the place.

Netleaf Hackberry

Our camp was a place of horses and cattle, barbed wire, worn trails, and abandoned mines. Instead of pine trees we had twisted mesquite, prickly pear cactus, and insidious, thigh-raking catclaw shrubs. The only trees that offered shade were appropriately called hackberry. The sun regularly hammered the desert hills with 100 degree temperatures. The humidity during the monsoons soured clothes in less than a day. But I loved it. How Karen managed those summers at camp in her gravid condition I never did try to understand.

Karen had conceived that spring after a day hike to the wind cave at Usery Mountain Park near our house in Mesa,

Arizona. It was her idea, both the hike and the romance, but she hadn't intended to get pregnant. Another child, she reasoned, would be inconvenient and might interfere with our traveling lifestyle. Babies rarely bring couples together. As early as the spring of 1986, Karen had begun to notice some growing problems with our marriage.

To Karen, I seemed preoccupied, stressed about trivial things: our straining financial situation, my career. It's not that these things weren't important, she just couldn't understand why they should drive me into sullen moods. It wasn't that serious. Karen saw me using activity to escape the pressure at home. I organized projects after school to fill days and science club trips to fill weekends, crowding my calendar those last few months before summer. I spent more time with my students than with my family. What Karen didn't see, or at least dismissed as a hormonal figment of her pregnancy, was that one particular student among all the others was present at every activity I planned and led.

When she came to camp at the end of June, I accepted it as fate. I was losing control; my life would never be the same. (Somehow, I believed it was only *my* life.) Our relationship would certainly escalate, but to what end I couldn't imagine. I had suggested to the camp director that he hire her as a special programs person to care for the children of some of the staff. He agreed, mostly because Karen was having trouble with her pregnancy and needed the extra help with our two little girls. I was no help. Camp can be a twenty-four-hour-a-day job, and I made it look like I had buried myself into it. I rarely slept but felt energized, indestructible. I couldn't eat and began losing weight. Physically, I was a wreck but I was feeling something I'd never experienced before, a kind of hypersensitivity and awareness. My wife and friends noticed the changes in me. So did the camp staff I supervised. I grew impatient with people, irrational and distant. I simply didn't care about anything except pursuing the source of my feelings—an illicit relationship with someone half my age, underage. After my arrest, the camp director told me he was relieved to find out my problem was another woman. He had thought I was turning into a jerk.

I was worse. Karen needed me, but I was focused on someone else. As the summer progressed, and I continued to regress, the staff began to make jokes about it, indirect criticism on how I treated my wife. Rumors circulated—someone had seen us together after midnight curfew. Peoples' ridicule reinforced my need to further escape reality, my responsibilities. I was living in an adolescent fantasy, and it made sense to me. My emotions dictated my behavior, and as they intensified, I became more and more obsessed. I believed I had gone beyond the point of no return.

Running away with her was the only choice I had. She, too, was distraught. She could no longer share me with my wife. "How do you think I feel when you go home to her every night after being with me?" I hadn't considered this. "What's going to happen to us after the summer is over?" I hadn't thought about it. I wasn't thinking about the next day much less the next months. I wanted our relationship to remain as it was, an affair. But she wanted more—or nothing at all.

On the morning of August fifth we left camp together for our day off. Before daylight, I packed my truck with a few camping supplies and some extra clothes. Then, before driving away, I stroked the swollen belly of my drowsy wife and hugged our children. I was having regrets but didn't know what else to do. I watched them sleep until it grew light and then left them, thinking I would never see them again. How I could do that I'll never understand. We spoke little during the two-hour drive to my home in Mesa. Once there, I gathered more belongings, dug up potatoes from the garden Karen and I had planted that spring, and fed our tropical fish, a pair of giant tiger oscars. I felt confused, uncertain. I was stalling, hoping that I could come to a decision. It came while I was lying on the couch, staring out the window. She stroked my damp forehead and said, "I know we can make it together." Hours later, heading away from Arizona, we drove into a cooling, mountain rainstorm. We both felt the relief. She said she got worried when it looked like I had changed my mind. I said a weight had lifted. I was free.

We toured the mining and resort towns of Colorado like a young couple on vacation. We had no plans except being together and spent our days sightseeing, fishing, and berry-picking. In Aspen, after two weeks, money ran low and I began looking for work. There, another teacher from Mesa recognized us in a bookstore and called the police.

She went back to school that fall, while I dealt with county jails, investigating officers, bond restrictions and judges, lawyers and reporters, people I had betrayed—coworkers, friends, my wife and children, to list the ones closest to me. My fantasy had erupted and had begun to shred lives. I had devastated everyone once precious to me, but it still didn't matter. I grieved only for my lost relationship with her. As a husband and father, as a human being, I was despicable.

Then in December, while on bond-release until my court date, Melissa was born. Her birth was my turning point. Setting aside her own feelings, her humiliation and rage, Karen had decided to salvage our marriage. Regardless of my behavior, despite that she would never go back to the camp chapel where she made them, her vows remained. For the months following my arrest in Colorado, Karen worked to bring me to my senses, confronting me with her pregnancy, our family, and the grave consequences I had caused us. She reminded me that I had responsibilities to her and our children regardless of the circumstances or the way I felt. She wanted me present when the baby came. The evening after Melissa's birth reality settled in. I discovered I could make decisions independent of how I felt about them. Standing over my new child and watching her sleep I took back a bit of control. I didn't have to walk away. I recognized I could return to my family.

Months afterward my emotions still plagued me, but I held onto my decision. I had come to my senses, although I was on my way to prison.

⊱┄◆┄○┄◆┄⊰

Outside my cell window the wind teethes on an empty soda can, spinning it in place where it's trapped in a corner of the building. It's been ten years. Prison keeps past events as fresh as ever. Tonight I'm writing about them as though they happened yesterday, convincing myself it's good therapy. It's strange how prison confines me, beyond the physical sense, even down to something as ephemeral as time. I try not to be bitter about it, to learn humility from the humiliation, strength from the severity. I hope that in this unholy place I may discover what is sacred to me—things like a letter from my daughter I read with regrets.

Harris' Hawk

When I get out, Kasondra wants me to teach her how to train hawks for hunting. She writes about this often. She would like to see me work with Harris' hawks again, and she wants a kestrel for herself. But even her mention of falconry rubs my face in the mess I've made of our lives. Unbidden, the memories of Jeremiah come, a Harris' hawk Karen and I had caught and trained in early 1986. We taught him to fly between us, from one fist to another, entirely free, as a daily routine for exercise. When hunting in the desert next to our home, he would respond to either one of us, and I remember how it thrilled me to watch him come to Karen's raised glove and to see the smile on her face. Working with Jeremiah was demanding, time consuming. But he bound us together as if by the cord he strung between us during his early, uncertain flights. As summer approached, and I no longer cared to invest the time in either the bird or my wife, I decided to release Jeremiah back to the wild. It was an accident of circumstance that I didn't tell Karen, so I convinced myself later. I'd forgotten about it, perhaps. Or she didn't remember my mentioning it. I could justify anything. What began as a couple, I ended with an act of separation, of distance. Jeremiah belonged to Karen, too. He was our bird, a part of our lives. He should have returned to the desert from her hand. Instead, it was a younger hand that let him go.

Tarantula

After a twenty-minute thunderstorm, I walk the sun down until even the eastern sky ignites with evening's violet mesentary. My feet crunch on wet gruss, the decomposed granite substrate of my world that's textured like Grape-Nuts cereal. The air is cool, heavy with breath, and swells like reconciliation—fresh, new, something undeserved.

Alongside the track some men have gathered to visit the home of a spider. It's become a regular attraction, and lately I've caught my eyes straying to the half-dollar-sized hole while making my circuits. Tonight, something well upholstered is out. When I approach I can see the heavy blond body of a female. She spans her burrow easily. In fact, she could fill the palm of my hand.

One of the men tosses her a giant beetle. She's instantly upon it, her fangs piercing its armor with a primeval sound, a sound out of the Devonian.

Despite this performance, I know that tarantulas are really quite gentle, hesitant to bite (non-beetles, anyway) unless provoked. And even then, the worst the spider may do is to kick a patch of barbed hairs off its abdomen in an attempt to irritate the eyes of its attacker.

The tarantula retreats into her hole and her audience begins to lose interest. When not hand-fed, she will lay out a network of silk threads from the den's entrance to cue her to the approach of potential prey, a kind of motion detector not unlike the prison's security system. She will also clear the surrounding area of debris as meticulously as the guards rake the perimeter sand traps.

Later, I encounter another tarantula, this one thin and anxious, a male out searching for a mate. The rain has stirred him to this seasonal ritual, and I can almost sense his urgency. A female lives up to twenty years and can afford to wait patiently in her burrow. Not so the male. He must have priorities. I've seen males so focused on engaging females that they shrink to little more than hairy bent spokes and sex drive.

Spider sex can be a matter of life and death. If he doesn't succumb to starvation, the male tarantula, when he locates a mate, must do more than just woo her. He must take, shall I say, precautions. After the introductory drumming of his pedipalps and some experimental touching, he squares off with her head to head. Over and over the pair rears up together in the universal posturing of love and aggression. When he's ready to make his move, he parries her fangs with special hooks on his forelegs, bends her backward, and slips his sperm-laden palps into her reproductive groove. He then scrambles for his life before his body becomes nourishment for her eggs.

Looking at life from the perspective of a spider can be sobering, particularly the perspective of a lonely, wandering male tarantula. (I wonder whether male chauvinism wouldn't be diminished if people were more like spiders in certain respects.) I consider carrying this one to the female's den, but he's agitated. He immediately flicks hair at me. I leave him on the track, alone with his post-storm lust. It's a fitting frustration for prison dwellers anyway.

Conenose Bugs

Six PM. The park. A late sun is in my eyes, its bright bulb stalled over the horizon causing the western sky to hemorrhage before nightfall. Birds scream in the trees: Brewer's blackbirds, house sparrows, and great-tailed grackles mass for an evening bitch session. Bird decibels. They complain loudly and all at once like those rabbinical street debates where volume is just as important as a good argument. The grackles, hidden in the dark plumage of the peppertrees, sound off above the others. Their piercing squeals sound like air escaping from the stretched lips of balloons.

The park is a sylvan oasis in the center of the prison yard. It is an eclectic gathering of vegetation, both native and exotic, the feral remnants of a long-cancelled horticulture course and its dismantled greenhouse. A water fountain and four picnic tables sit in a grassy rectangle sectioned by several wide, rose-bordered paths. This is the only order to the park. Among the tables and paths, trees and shrubs attempt a pattern with no particular plan. The largest are peppertrees and desert willow, and they stand out against a single, odd eucalyptus and china-berry tree. Beneath these, bonsai-pruned privet, Texas ranger, catclaw, jojoba, rose, and Mexican bird of paradise enclose

Jojoba

flower beds of marigold, iris, geranium, zinnia, mint, and spider plant. The greenhouse wasn't dismantled. It exploded.

Desert willow, jojoba, and catclaw are the only natives in the park. But even cultivated and dressed to the point of looking like ornamentals in a Japanese garden (the landscape crews won't allow so much as a blade of grass to become unruly, much less a few desert plants), they still resemble their wild counterparts. The catclaw particularly, those hard, brutal shrubs that guard the fringes of desert arroyos. Catclaw. The name refers to the tiny sharp hooks that reach out across open space to tattoo bare skin. The shrubs don't have branches; they have paws and, in my mind, they demand as much respect as cacti.

As I began to write more and more about the desert beyond

the fences, relying initially on experiences from my childhood and with my family, these native plants on the yard
grew in importance. It helped me to actually see and smell
and touch the subjects of my essays, of their accompanying
illustrations especially. Consequently, I started making notes
on the yard's natives, from the most insignificant "weeds" to
the more obvious trees and cacti. Walking the track each day
for exercise I scanned the base of the perimeter fence, an area
beyond the incessant razing of the work crew's rakes and
hoes. There, I discovered flue-stemmed skeleton weeds and
ground-clutching *Euphorbias,* the latter relatives of Christmas
poinsettias.

I picked wildflowers such as fetid marigold and desert
zinnia, sometimes poking a hand through the fence to get to
them. The bookshelf in my cell expanded to include wild-
flower guides and keys to southwestern plants. My notebook
filled out with sketches and notes and pressed plant parts:
ocotillo in front of Dining Area One, desert willow in the
park, yucca on Yard Four, prickly pear at the Indian sweat
lodge, mesquite in the Administrative Area, barrel cactus, century plant, Mexican paloverde. I found a surprising variety. I
even managed to keep track of the saguaro, prickly pear, and
cholla in the cactus garden at the entrance to the Santa Rita
Unit, recording the time and length of their flowering and
fruiting seasons. In the evenings I could smell the saguaro
fruit in the heat of ripening—a sweet odor like strawberry
wine vomit. The prison yard was mostly dirt, Bermuda grass,
and greenhouse exotics, but I could still tune myself with the
desert and let it teach me. In fact, much of what I learned
about the desert, and much of what went into my natural
history articles and pen and ink drawings for magazines like

Prickly Pear Cactus

Jumping Cholla

New Mexico Wildlife (a publication our prison library first introduced me to), *Arizona Great Outdoors,* and *Arizona Highways,* came from my observations and studies in prison.

⊱──•◦•──⊰

Six-thirty PM. Gloaming comes. Soon the moon will rise and eclipse for the last time this century. I suppose I'll watch it with the others, though I've seen it many times already. The park fades with the twilight and the birds lapse into quiet. Bats screen the air for insects, curling in and out of the trees on ragged leather wings. Western pipistrelles and big browns. A hawkmoth circles a bird of paradise near me, darting into the flower bracts like a hummingbird insomniac. White-lined sphinx moths are common nighttime visitors and often mistaken for hummingbirds because of their similar size and flight characteristics. They also love nectar, favoring the nocturnally fragrant blooms of plants like sacred datura and night-blooming cereus. I can just hear the flutter of wings, an unexpected sound coming from a furze-coated moth.

The park is a great place for bug watching. Here, I've seen honeybees drenched with the semen of marigolds; black, lumbering carpenter bees lay siege to delicate desert willow blossoms while, nearby, swallowtail butterflies probe the flowers' narrow necks. I've watched tarantula hawks, their red wings flicking, march through the grass tracking their spider prey, and pinacate beetles trudge along in the same way seemingly without any purpose. On hot afternoons robberflies patrol the airspace for succulent insect snacks (fast food on the wing) and roadside skippers hover in jagged holding patterns over wet ground. Occasionally, a cicada will sing its heavy metal serenade for a voiceless mate,

Pinacate Beetle

which is for me the call of summer. Nearly year-round this park is a blooming, buzzing, cackling, pungent menagerie. It beats and breathes and bleeds with life in the center of this lifeless impoundment.

At the edge of the park the harvester ants are getting settled for bed. Only a few are out. One, a dedicated, half-inch worker, hauls one last corkscrew seed to its nest, dragging it backward toward a nickel-sized hole in the ground. Seed-husks and crumpled ants rim a craterlet of peppered sand.

Although I sometimes feed them fat hornworm caterpillars and grasshoppers, seeds are the harvesters' principal food. Workers have a beardlike basket under their chins for carting the seeds of grasses and flowers—here, peppergrass, marigold, filaree—to their nests. But seed foragers are only part of this all-female, caste society. The sorority also comprises nest-building masons, seed-husking millers, grub-raising nurses, and the queen's attendants. Males have no other role than to fertilize the queen and die. The queen, however, is not the focus of the colony. She has two functions: eating and reproducing. It's her eggs and larvae that the entire colony, which can number several thousand, centers on. Not only are they the future workforce, but the larvae are the colony's collective stomach. After nurse-workers feed them chewed seeds, the grubs digest and then regurgitate food for all the adults. Everyone eats baby vomit.

I love to check out the harvester ants after the summer monsoons bring the first hard rain. For them, the storm is a breeding trigger. I've seen worker ants forcibly drag the winged alates to the surface of the nest and release them all at once—a shuddering cloud of sex drive evaporating into the air.

Harvester Ants

A nuptial frenzy commences as winged males, outnumbering females five to one, congregate at an elevated area like a hilltop creosote bush. Here, males release a chemical to attract females, but other males also cue on the sexual signal. The frenzy escalates as swarms of male ants perfume the air and scour the rendezvous site for a few rare females. Competition is intense. A female ant has her pick of suitors, and often she will cause several to fight among themselves, each scrambling for a chance to inseminate her. Aggressive mating like this can lead to bizarre consequences. During copulation a male may bite his partner in half as he grips her with his mandibles while other males attempt to pry him off. Even stranger, a female will sometimes sever her overzealous mate's abdomen. If the body part remains attached to her, the sacrificed male may actually benefit reproductively by preventing rivals from diluting his sperm; the queen's new colony will be his descendants alone. His death is insignificant; once fertilized, the queen has no further need of him.

Civilization and sex. Who would've guessed that these diminutive subsurface plows could have such a full life just beneath our feet? I wonder if the ants mind being in prison. Probably not, since their whole world sinks maybe six feet underground and radiates overland as much as 130 feet. There is plenty of room here for ants. Thinking about our resident harvester ants I cannot escape noticing the parallelism. We, too, live in subterranean (at least partially) masonry cells, a single-sexed, non-reproducing horde of workers who unwillingly serve a colony. Inmate construction workers built this prison. Inmate farmers and cooks and waste disposal crews keep it running. Mindlessness is our instinct. We obey without thinking, doing as we're told, sustaining a system that exists to devour budgets and breed an even larger workforce of mindless slaves. Our queen also has two similar functions focusing on eating and reproducing. When we are no longer of any value to her, we are released, discarded on the perimeter as crushed and lifeless husks. But the colony thrives.

I admit I've captured a few harvester ants and glued their little legs to postcards to immobilize them so I could draw them. I've asphyxiated one or two moths, too, for the same reason, and maybe a few more butterflies. Butterflies, with their colorful, sequined wings, have a higher value as greeting cards than as pen and ink drawings, so some have told me.

In February when the days grow warm and green spears push up the dark soil in the park's flower beds, a friend of mine named Dave starts talking about the flowers—and the butterflies lured to them. Dave has access to sheets of clear laminate, a self-sticking plastic used to protect books and documents or line kitchen shelves. It comes in a heavy roll from Boise Cascade and the library always has remnants, available from the inmate clerks for a price (cigarettes or sodas). For him, the clear plastic is gold. Using a single-edged razor blade—serious contraband—he cuts the rolled plastic into four- or six-inch squares. As the flowers and butterflies arrive Dave sorts them into a plant press made of cardboard and paper towels and crunches them under stacked cases of paper in the education office. In the park I've helped Dave capture monarchs, swallowtails, and sulphur butterflies, netting them with our hands or by throwing our shirts at them. We've also picked flowers for pressing: poppy, rose, yellow columbine, carnation, and baby's breath. After two weeks of pressing and drying, Dave arranges a tiny bouquet of color with a single butterfly on one sticky surface of the plastic and

Prickly Poppy

then seals it with a second square. Each is a perfect natural greeting card, a sample of our prison spring that Dave sells for five or ten postage stamps. My daughters have a collection of them, signed by me on all the birthdays and Valentine's Days I've missed. Aside from the few butterfly collectors, inmates generally treat the insects and spiders that inhabit the park with indifference, which is, in reality, a kind of respect. Some will make pets of the more unusual arachnids, such as scorpions and tarantulas, keeping them in a shoebox and feeding them crickets. Tarantulas do get some attention when they show up after the summer rains, shuffling along with that cautious but precise, eight-legged gait. Males, I understand, hunting for females. I think the fascination with scorpions and tarantulas is the brutal way they overpower other small animals and make meals of them. Scorpions have nearly indefensible weaponry in their sting and its flesh-searing toxin. Tarantulas have toxin too, delivered through a pair of black hollow fangs unfolding from under a body that spans an adult hand. Grasshoppers, crickets, June beetles, even small mice don't stand a chance.

I can identify with this attraction for venomous animals with nasty eating habits. I've kept black widows and tarantulas as pets. One of my favorites, the sun spider, or solpugid, has the largest jaws relative to body size of any animal in the world. This straw-colored arachnid looks like a scorpion but is much quicker and, instead of pincers, has forward appendages called pedipalps that are forever sweeping, tapping, touching the ground, as if the spider were a blind man with a pair of canes. It is not sightless, however, and it is a formidable hunter.

Recently, I prodded one with a finger and it aggressively attacked me, seemingly unconcerned about my size. I wanted to watch it feed, and so I dumped it into a plastic container and chased down a cricket, a scene that got the attention of two guards. (It turned out they were as interested in seeing the solpugid eat as I was.) The spider killed the cricket instantly with a terrific bite and then began to tear into its abdomen. It worked both its paired, needlelike fangs in tandem, the upper two sawing with the lower two, causing the spider's entire head to pump like a piston engine. I could hear the spider cracking into the cricket as would a seafood aficionado with a Maine lobster. Eight legs drove the jaws deeper into the body until after a half hour it was a shrunken husk, twisted upon itself, head bent unnaturally to one side. When it was over, the noticeably fatter sun spider flexed its jaws to clean them, reminding me of how a hawk strops its beak after devouring a fresh kill.

Six-fifty PM. A flock of birds explodes out of one of the peppertrees, startling several inmates walking beneath it. They duck their heads and spin toward the fleeing birds as if to confront an assailant. The main yard is closing. A voice from a loud speaker orders us to return to our respective areas, one of four fenced yards, each with a housing unit of ninety-six two-man cells. The field lights have come on, washing out the darkening sky to a tobacco-smoke haze and spoiling any star-gazing on my walk back. Only light from the brightest stars and planets can sift through; tonight, Arcturus in the west and Jupiter in the south, but the lights bring other things into view. A nighthawk threads through a nearby tent of light where insects swarm like plankton. Beetles in medieval armor drop out of the soup, smacking and skitter-

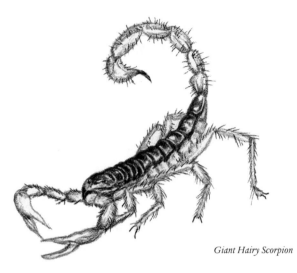

Giant Hairy Scorpion

ing against the concrete basketball court. They distract me. I want to know what they are, and I chase them down. A pinacate beetle douses my fingers with a stench that won't rub off.

At the eastern end of the yard dozens of men are gathering to witness the lunar eclipse. Many sit in the grass, smoking, drinking sodas; others stand around in groups of three or five and talk quietly among themselves. I join them and feel their expectation. It's like a holy event. Above the eastern horizon the moon is nearly eclipsed, only a bright sunlit cap remains. The earth's shadow eats at the moon from below, the blackness racing through space to chase it down as it rises over our heads. I'm thinking about the speed of shadow versus the speed of light when the moon falls into shade and begins to glow an unearthly copper. Someone in front of me says, "It's like we're standing on another planet with a strange moon."

I tire of the eclipse. I've seen several solar and at least half a dozen lunar eclipses from behind these fences. It's always a spectacle; even the guards come out of their control rooms to see them. For solar eclipses I construct shadow boxes for the inmates I teach. Others view them through welding masks, smoked glass, and photographic film and marvel at the dimming daylight, the blurred edges of shadows, until the sun's penumbra slides past us. But it's getting old. I can't remember ever seeing an eclipse, lunar or solar, outside this prison.

In a place where boredom can be refined to a new level, where even celestial events can get tedious, I'd rather watch bugs. I'd rather marvel at the sexual appetites of ants, the muscle-generating warm-bloodedness of hawkmoths, the heat-indifference of sweating cicadas. I've heard a man could spend a lifetime studying just one or two of the many undescribed beetles on the planet. The last time I talked to Gene Hall, an entomologist at the University of Arizona working on describing new beetles in the Southwest, he told me sixteen species had been discovered in the previous eighteen months just in Arizona. "Definitely the best state in the country for insects," he said. My guidebook to insects of the Southwest mentions several kinds that little is known about, insect species I've seen right here. Like our many kinds of darkling beetles for instance. What do they eat? How, when, and where do the larvae feed? What is a suitable forage stand? What is the winter survivorship and how does the population fluctuate with climatic factors? What is the natural range? So many questions. I'm thinking I could do life with the bugs.

Sun Spider

Sonoran Desert Toad

I wait in line for my weekly shopping at the inmate commissary and watch a man with a toad in his hands. We had rain this morning, a tremendous predawn thunderstorm of the kind that never fails to keep the prison yard on lockdown. Wind and rain blurred the perimeter lights while lightning threatened to shut down the power system altogether. It was weather for toads. Later, after the storm passed and we were allowed to begin our day, I crossed the yard, navigating chocolate pools and streamlets to pick up my bag of groceries. Today: coffee, a loaf of wheat bread, a jar of crunchy peanut butter, plastic hangers, and some writing materials.

The inmate had found the toad where it breached the flooded Bermuda in a low area between the store and the classrooms. Now, he cradles it as he would a letter from a wife, or a photo of his baby girl. The two seem to communicate a mutual fascination. One captive to another. It's a benevolent scene, and an unlikely one on this gray day wet with humidity and sweat. At the head of the line a guard notices the scene too, but his face is contorted. It is a hard look, disguised of humanity. *This is prison,* it says. In mock concern for the animal he shouts, "Put the frog down! It's done nothing to you!" Oh, but it has, I think. It's charmed him, here in the middle of this desperate place. And maybe for a moment, he's escaped into the memory of something—a childhood pet and playmate, perhaps. I guess this from the way, even now, he watches the toad back in the grass. And the look of his vague but plain smile.

⋙─┼─◆─○─◆─┼─⋘

I dig for a toad in the visitation sandbox, to the expectation and delight of my daughters. The amphibian is huge—a Sonoran desert toad—and wedged tightly under the concrete sidewalk. I stick my hand into the dark and clamp down on its head. It has no neck. I work my fingers like forceps laboring against a stubborn birth. The toad puffs itself up and digs in. It won't come easily. I am nervous about it. The guards wrote up an inmate last week for doing what I'm doing. They said he was stashing drugs; he insisted that wasn't the case, that his kids said something was moving down in the sandy hole. Disciplinary court couldn't find him guilty without any evidence, but he still spent several days in the "hole" on investigative lockdown. Solitary confinement. It's like going to prison in a prison.

It takes both hands to hold the toad. It bucks and squirms and finally empties its bladder over my fingers and my girls jump back and scream. "It's just water," I tell them. "It's normal. It wants me to let it go." I put the toad down in the sandbox and the girls encircle it. Karen watches for the guards, concerned they might disapprove. Animals can be unpredictable and the guards insist on control. The toads are deadly, too, so they inform us every time one appears and they notice our interest.

The toad lifts itself on stubby legs and moves forward one body length. This is not what I would consider a hop, more like a push. The girls back away but keep an interested perimeter. It pushes again. It's all warts and eyes, the latter like clear golden beads attached to an ugly green bag of liquid. Melissa, blond, blue-eyed, and my youngest, can't handle it anymore. She climbs into the arms of her mother and complains, "It's staring at me. It's staring at me."

It's possible that the inmate the guards wrote up *was* stashing drugs. I know people on this yard who lick toads for the intoxicating effects. As a defense, Sonoran desert toads secrete a toxic milk from large glands behind each eye. The poison can cause temporary but violent fits and paralysis in coyotes and dogs, when the animals bite or chew on the toads. Unless you stick a finger in an eye after handling one, the toads aren't harmful to people. And, licking the slime-laden warts will only make you sick, not high. Those who know what they're doing don't lick toads, they smoke them. Burning the poison and then inhaling it can send the smoker on an intense hallucinogenic mind-warp not unlike that produced by LSD. Toad-smoking aficionados, a growing subculture even outside of prison, don't actually harm the toads. They squeeze the glands to collect the poison, then dry it and mix it with tobacco (toad rollies) or burn it in a pipe.

I've never smoked a toad before, but I've tasted the toxin. It's as tongue-numbing as Novocain. If inhaling the smoke is as mind-numbing, I can understand why the toads attract some prisoners. They are a way out of this place. They are ugly, green bags of chemical-induced freedom. Toads, however, offer more than drugs in relief from walls and bars.

On warm evenings Sonoran desert toads the size of

grapefruits wait for darkness in the shrubbery outside our cells. Lights attract insects, which attract toads. Occasionally men will gather around with guitars and sing lonely ballads about unfaithful wives or distant girlfriends. Mexican music prevails, which seems most appropriate for this place. As the toads appear, the men catch beetles to feed them. When they run out of beetles, they'll toss crickets, scorpions, ripe olives, even juvenile toads. The cannibals snap up everything that moves, including lighted cigarette butts. This offering the toads reject, backing away, drawing in their eyes, scraping their tongues with tiny hands. A cruel form of amusement but not the worst. I've seen the blackened, twisted bodies of giant toads dangling lifeless from curls of razor wire, as if a shrike had made its larder there.

The toad in the visitation sandbox patiently humors my girls as they construct ponds, walls, and castles for it to live in. Then, finally, it escapes and dives into its underground chamber. I can't blame it. As comfortable and protective as enclosures may be, prison still makes me want to burrow underground like a toad. We leave it alone for now.

I came to prison when Jessica was four years old, Kasondra, two, and Melissa only a few months. Melissa took her first steps in prison visitation. I knew I would be at most just a weekend presence in their lives, hardly a father except by title. I wanted to influence my children as much as possible. They were already too much like their mother: blond, lithe, intelligent ... girls. Not that this is a bad thing, of course. Still, they carry half my genes, even if it doesn't show. They would need me, I reasoned, to balance their dolls with balls, their ribbons and bows with insects and toads.

Great Plains Toad

From the beginning, I took them on missions for toads in the visitation park, a large enclosure of trees, grass, and picnic tables attached to the main visitation area that now stands idle, unused, although it's kept neatly landscaped. We searched for them in the deep grass of a drainage ditch, beneath oil drums used as garbage cans, and along a dirt strip at the perimeter fence. Most were small Sonoran desert toads and Great Plains toads. Occasionally, we'd uncover a spadefoot. My daughters would fill the pockets of their Osh Kosh overalls with the cool, thumb-sized nuggets of juvenile activity and laugh as the toads chirped rapid fire complaints from under their clothing. They had bold intentions of smuggling them home. Little criminals. Typically, however, they would rebury their bug-eyed jewels in the sandbox, and then look for them from week to week and, often as not, locate them again. Digging up toads in visitation was our game. Other fathers played Checkers or Scrabble with their kids; we went hunting for buried treasure.

Nature writer Christine Colasurdo says we live on one layer of the earth at a time. It just happens that my one layer has razor wire horizons. Despite this, I still wanted my love for wilderness to seep into my children. Prison wouldn't last forever, and I looked forward to a time when we could all go camping and hiking and fishing, things I missed sorely and hoped to share with them. I wanted them to accept the whole experience of wilderness, too, not the window-seat tour but the *adventure,* the dirt, sweat, and hunger. I would bait their hooks as long as the girls would deal with mosquito bites and cold, wet feet.

Until then, I could prepare them with whatever bits of grace prison sent us, bits like toads. For now, the toads in visitation would be our way to wilderness, a squirming, hand-held means for me to connect my children to nature. I couldn't be sure where it would lead. But as toads moved into the girls' bedroom and became pets, science projects, and essays, I felt less concern about balance in their lives.

Then came my miraculous (if temporary) release, and that one summer my daughters and I found the spadefoot toads. The previous December, after serving nearly eight years of my twelve-year sentence, a superior court judge overturned my conviction and sent me home to my family. The decision didn't come easy, not for the judge and not for my wife and lawyers. After I went to prison, Karen, while caring for our then small daughters, went back to school to study criminal law. She specialized in legislative histories, focusing on the law behind my crime. She researched the similar statutes of other states and met with legislators. She spoke at conferences, appeared on radio talk shows locally and television talk shows nationally. When her political efforts paid off in some changes in the law, my investigating officer approached the Pinal County Attorney and requested that my sentence be reconsidered. The way my case had been handled had disturbed him and he offered to testify on my behalf. Karen sought out a law firm to work with the County Attorney in arranging a resentencing under the new laws. Karen's work impressed the Sherick Law Firm, who agreed to take me on as a pro bono client and later hired my wife as a paralegal. What's most amazing to me still is Karen's response to my crime. She could have divorced me, an understandable reaction to behavior like mine. I had humiliated her publicly, betrayed her in the worst way a man can betray a woman, a husband a wife.

The judge took three months to make his decision, basing it on two days of testimony at my hearing for post-conviction relief. Evidence the state had collected to originally convict me—together with new testimony, including that of both investigating officers—my attorneys now used to win my release. At my resentencing, the judge said it was time for all of us to move on with our lives. He placed me on probation for the remainder of my sentence and allowed me to go home. Unfortunately, the Arizona Court of Appeals would not agree with him. Eighteen months after my prosecutor appealed the decision, three justices ordered my return to prison. The appellate court does not go easy on sex offenders.

The first summer of my temporary release the monsoon season began with a terrific thunderstorm, which darkened most of Tucson late one afternoon. The wind came first, raising sheets of dust and sticking leaves and twigs to window panes that rattled and vibrated as if to loosen the debris. As the wind finished its choking assault, it charged in with rain, stinging rain, huge, pelting, steel-ball-bearing rain, rain that cratered the ground and tore it away in muddy streams. For most of the year the arroyo in our backyard is only sand—bright, eye-squinting quartz grit. But on this afternoon the wash raged with mud and foam and uprooted vegetation carried by the afterbirth of the storm.

By evening, the water had receded and the spadefoot toads began calling out in the post-storm quiet. Theirs were the cries of motherless lambs, urgent, as if they understood the dictates of shrinking pools in the desert.

My daughters were nervous about leaving the house after the storm, particularly after dark. But the toads drew them. Something mysterious was happening down at the arroyo; we could hear it through the drizzle. I held onto a flashlight and dip net while the girls clung to my arms, and we worked our way down the road and up the wash. Shrubs and grasses, bent and torn, betrayed the recent passage of the floodwater as if some enormous snake had just slid past us. But the wash was now only a broken chain of pools. We found the spadefoots in a truck-sized hole gouged out of the wash by the storm runoff and then filled with muddy water. I slipped into the pool, sinking waist-deep, and netted the first pair of toads I saw locked in amplexus. We quickly returned to the girls' aquarium and released the mating toads. In the morning we freed them, but not before they left us with a mass of fertilized eggs, hundreds of tiny black beads suspended in clear jelly.

This was the summer we discovered that spadefoot toads are one of the desert's miracles. For years they rest underground, barely alive, escaping a hot, dry landscape that would otherwise reduce them to wood chips. We learned that in this state they eat nothing. They drink nothing, storing a third of their body weight in water in canteenlike bladders. For most of their lives the amphibians are mere seeds. Then, awakened by the deep, pounding rhythm of a summer thunderstorm, they emerge en masse to breed. It's as if the right mixture of water and sand produces toads by spontaneous generation.

The eggs in my daughters' aquarium began hatching in less than thirty-six hours, each tadpole spinning and kicking within a clear capsule, fighting to free itself from the jelly. We estimated that we had more than eight hundred tadpoles, tiny wrigglers all head, gills, and tail. In the arroyo, the pool was sinking into the sand, marooning globs of eggs on its banks like spilled caviar drying in the sun. But many of the eggs had hatched, and thousands of black commas punctuated the tea-stained water.

We had read that spadefoot toads are record holders for metamorphosis. Normally, it takes them about two to six weeks to change from hatchling to toadlet, depending on factors such as water temperature and available food. But we also knew that the tadpoles could adjust their growth according to the duration of their pond when it isn't too crowded. If the alternative is getting baked into the mud curls at the bottom of a puddle, the tadpoles can sprout limbs and crawl onto land in fewer than ten days. Sometimes, this might be the only way to survive an unpredictable desert pond.

With this information, the girls decided to keep a notebook to record the tadpoles' metamorphosis, comparing those tadpoles in their aquarium with those in the arroyo and logging the differences in temperature. Our adventure was becoming a science project. Their notes are interesting if not entirely conclusive. In less than a day the girls' tadpoles had doubled in size. In five days they were as big as peas; after six they had hind-leg buds. At ten days the tadpoles' round bodies had deflated into lumpy toad forms, front and hind limbs flexing new muscles as their tails dwindled. As they grew from swimmers to floaters, my daughters scooped them up and placed them into a terrarium.

The pond in the arroyo had been shrinking steadily since the storm, the tadpoles there becoming frantic with motion as the temperature increased and the borders of their world descended upon them. At eight days the pool was a roiling vat of tadpole soup. On the ninth day it was gone. The girls wrote that when they approached the place, dozens of small toads hopped across the wet sand, dragging limp tails behind them.

It was interesting for us to notice that the spadefoot frenzy in our wash coincided with the emergence of a congress of insects. Most significantly, the thunderstorms had triggered termites. On the same evening when the amphibians had pushed to the surface to begin their mating and egg-laying cycle, hordes of winged termites boiled out of their nests for their aerial nuptials. Termites are small packages rich in fat, enough calories in one or two nights' gorging to ready the toads for their long sleep and instantaneous fertility.

Melissa discovered that not only were termites easy to find and collect but that baby toads relish them. The toads targeted on the white, moving bodies, lapping them up with tiny sticky tongues. As the toadlets quickly grew, the girls fed them larger and larger fare—ants, sow bugs, beetle grubs. By the end of summer they had the toads accustomed to gulping down tangled knots of pet store blackworms served on a toothpick.

It's late October now, less than three months since my return to prison. A Pacific cold front is delivering its burden of cold

Couch's Spadefoot Toad

air and rain and wind, sticking the blackbirds to the ground and muddying the track. I haven't seen any swallows, those deciduous birds, for a few days. I suspect they've left on the leading edge of the storm, and already I miss the way they dip and cut across the Bermuda on razor-blade wings. Recently, we've had record highs in the eighties, and the swallows have been massing. I counted more than a hundred flying circles over the field, the most I'd ever seen here.

Today, a rare sight. A dozen or so ducks fly a perfect, south-pointing V against a concrete sky—a typical fall scene that seems misplaced in this desert.

Another rarity. Off to the side of the exercise track I find a toad. It's perfectly still when I pick it up, an ice cube in my hand. I recognize the squat, goblinlike amphibian immediately: bright yellow-green skin and swollen eyes. A Couch's spadefoot. It's alive; the eyes shine and I can see deep inside them. I carefully turn it over and look for its digging tools, the namesake black halfmoon "spades" on both hind feet.

Strange, I think, this cold weather toad. It should be deep underground. It's been a while since I've noticed any signs of them at the margin of the track, the pushed up mounds of dirt, like little impact craters, where spadefoots sink backward into the ground in slow spirals. This one must have been confused by the storm, the pounding rain, or perhaps the tremors of a passing delivery truck. I've heard that the deep vibrations of off-road vehicles can wake the toads out of season.

I spend the evening with the toad, thinking of my children and trying to sketch it. It won't cooperate. I can't tie it down as I've done with lizards, and the glue I've used on the feet of ants and beetles is out of the question. With my notebook in my lap and a pencil in one hand, I hold the creature between a thumb and three fingers as it warms and squirms under my desk lamp. Now it can see deep into my eyes. When its squirms turn into hiccups in staccato, I put down my pencil. The toad sings, filling my cell with the same passion expressed in those lonely Spanish ballads. It is the wisdom of more than just toads that companionship begins with song. But desire sometimes goes unheard and unanswered out of season. Or out of place.

I try not to think about this. Instead, I hold the toad and allow myself to listen to the wildness, the freedom in its voice. It's not an escape, more a kind of passage. It guides me to that nighttime foray with my girls where their small hands held those toads of summer.

Desert Tortoise

Summer is gone in one day. Overhead, a dark cloudspan seals off the sky in a solid, unmoving mass. A cold, gritty wind slaps against me as I walk my laps, an exercise of obsession that keeps me cutting a visible path near the perimeter fence the way a dog traces the borders of its pen. For one half of my circuit I push into the wind's dry and icy hands; for the other half the same hands push me along. Shove and be shoved. Charge and retreat. Around and around. The wind is a sadistic cop, a sadistic prison system. I complete four laps and I've had enough. There's a deep throbbing ache in my inner ears where the cold has penetrated from my exposed lobes by convection. My ear lobes might as well be made of aluminum for all their insulating properties.

Yesterday I sweated these same laps under a bright metallic blister that drove temperatures into the eighties. As the cold front elbowed its way into the Southwest, temperatures fell forty degrees in less than twenty-four hours. It's not uncommon. Weather extremes do occur here. At certain times of the year it's expected.

I've decided that if you intend to live in the desert you'll need the physiology of a reptile. Desert rats, with apologies to the late Edward Abbey (the quintessential desert rat), can't hack it. Pack rats, in fact, are wimps. Furry, goggle-eyed, thin-blooded wimps. To survive here they must construct elaborate nests of refuse to protect themselves from our region's climate. They retreat into their snug middens with every pulse of the mercury, just when the desert starts demanding attention.

Reptiles, on the other hand, adapt. Lizards and snakes, the cold-blooded denizens of this arid place, defy the worst conditions it can sling at them—floods and frost, desiccating winds and sweltering summer doldrums. When it gets cold they slow down (I like that), eating less, moving less, sleeping more. Torpor. A kind word. When it's hot they like it even better, composing themselves on shaded or sunlit surfaces to soak up the perfect body heat. Some lizards, like zebratails and desert iguanas, can tolerate body temperatures of 115 degrees, the highest among vertebrate animals. Reptiles are the desert's native rock, igneous basalt with scales. Desert rats are seasonal tourists by comparison.

Adaptability is the key: bending to the whims of a place where hypothermia and heat exhaustion can threaten you in the same day. Reptiles do it. In fact, there is probably no other animal better acclimated than our desert tortoise with its horny shell, armor-plated hide, and voluminous bladder —all water conservation devices. The bladder is an exceptional "canteen." Southwestern folklore tells of dying men being revived by drinking the contents of a tortoise's bladder. But there are others, plants particularly, that adapt just as well in their own way, that have adjusted to deal with the vagaries of this extreme land, vagaries like our seasons. We still call them by their traditional names—spring, summer, fall,

Blue Lupine

Mexican Goldpoppy

winter—but there's nothing traditional about them, especially summer. What most refer to as "summer" is too simplistic for our eight-month-long incandescent period. Some prefer to divide this period into three separate seasons: foresummer, monsoon summer, and aftersummer. Now we have six seasons. Okay. But there's more to handling this eccentric desert than changing the names of the seasons. On this low desert rangeland of creosote, mesquite, and cholla where the prison sprawls, spring slips in by mid-February. It is a silent approach, fairly unnoticed. All winter annual wildflowers have been preparing, pushing iceberg leaves across bare ground and storing up energy in roots and stems despite the cold. If we've had favorable moisture, dark green mounds of filaree will stain the stiff Bermuda. Bladderpod may thread its stems through the chain link. Sometimes, when I'm lucky, a rogue Mexican goldpoppy—one of the classic winter annuals— will stray onto the yard. All these bloom with the first touch of warmth, tiny lavender asterisks, yellow crosses, golden cups. Away from the prison, along roadsides, over creosote flats, on sloping bajadas, goldpoppies, together with their companion lupines, bathe the ground with royal colors. In a good year. Some springs, in the same place, you'd never guess there had been any flowers at all the previous season.

One of the ways winter annuals such as goldpoppy and lupine, desert chicory and bladderpod have adapted to our sometimes hostile environment is by producing tough seeds, seeds that don't germinate easily. Thick, hard seed coats that must pass through an animal's digestive tract or those that moisture-loving bacteria must dissolve can lock up a plant's germination for years until conditions are right for growth. In a desert where rainfall can vary widely from year to year, it won't do to have seeds sprout at the first sprinkle and then mummify within a week. Tough seed coats prevent that. I could learn about the value of a hard exterior in tune with its surroundings.

For several years—until the landscape crews finally cut them away—half a dozen or so brittlebushes struggled to overcome the caliche soil along the southern perimeter fence. Brittlebush, a native perennial shrub with backbone, generally begins a flowering thrust near the spring equinox following the reproductive peak of the annual wildflowers. I've seen them transform the foothills into a surging yellow tide in some years, less so in others, when they drop flowers, leaves, and stems and lie dormant, spindly skeletons among circlets of white, ashen litter. Even their roots are expendable, shrinking back while the plants wait for rain. Brittlebushes are patient opportunists. They have to be. And, although they no longer scent the air in the prison with their pungent resin, I still admire them for their expediency.

In April, foresummer bullies in with its high pressure and hot, sterile winds that send spring's verdure to seed and scatter butterflies like pressed and dried flower petals. It is a time when desert plants must prove themselves. Ignoring the drought, the toughest natives unveil an unexpected potency. Outside the fence, a single blue paloverde erupts with yellow blooms. The Mexican paloverdes across the yard follow, their flowers gathering and dropping and piling up like day-old buttered popcorn on the floor of a moviehouse. When our only mesquite tree unfurls its fuzzy yellow catkins, the prickly pear and cholla cacti join in, marking a flowering epiphany that mocks the heat. In the unit's cactus garden, creamy white bouquets crown every saguaro.

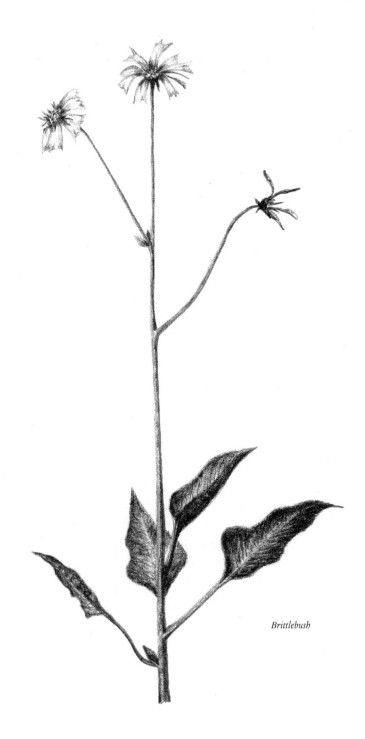

Brittlebush

Late in June consecutive days of 100-plus-degree temperatures are accumulating. Petals brown and drop, leaves wither, cacti pucker, even the tortoises retreat to their burrows. Only the cicada, whose jangled cadence grates on every nerve as a kind of auditory punctuation mark for the heat, don't seem to care. They'll keep warming up at 116 degrees. Foresummer allows the desert to purify itself. Resting under a woolen blanket of white heat, seeds bake, waiting for rain.

A curious thing happens at the height of the drought. The saguaros produce fruit. It is foresummer harvest for wildlife, a nourishing respite that comes when it's most needed. As the figlike *pitahayas* of the giant cactus ripen and peel open, spitting red pulp and gritty black seeds, white-winged and mourning doves, cactus wrens and curve-billed thrashers descend on the fruits. What they knock to the ground, squirrels and pocket mice devour, scattering thirsty beetles and gnats. Nothing is wasted. Harvester ants welcome the feast, single-filing away any misplaced seeds.

I like to say that I admire the saguaro. Our signature cactus. I say I appreciate it for its arrogance; it is a symbol of defiance in a hostile country. I suppose I attribute this attitude to the saguaro because I want to, because I can identify with it. But the saguaro isn't a rebellious prisoner, held against its will in some twisted environment. The saguaro accepts the desert for what it is, on its terms. It complies. It's in the plant's roots, shallow mats of tough rope that radiate out more than fifty feet to draw on only a few inches of moisture each year, in its spongy, accordion-pleated columns that hold those few inches, in its thick, waxy cuticle that protects them. The spines also, splayed from areolas along each rib, help conserve water by providing shade and creating pockets of insulating air while discouraging thirsty browsers. The saguaro likes it here, belongs here. It is a child of the desert.

In early July, the parched heat of foresummer soaks through with humidity. Weeks of high pressure over the Southwest have finally provoked moist air to circle in from the Gulf of Mexico. A threshold has been crossed. Monsoon winds have delivered their tropical package: rain. It is a violent delivery, and it breaks the grip of the foresummer drought in one afternoon. From the prison yard I watch clouds pile up all morning against the Catalina Mountains in the north, the Rincons in the east, and the Santa Ritas in the south. Late in the day thunderheads bruise the horizon, untying themselves to graze en masse across the intermountain basin. Then the wind comes. And comes. Colors fade, wash out. A terrific duststorm rides on a pressure wave of an intense but local thunderstorm; its target, seemingly, is this prison. Lockdown. Lightning and thunder arrive together, cracking open this cloud-darkened patch of desert. The storm dumps hail first, which jigs on the ground and pulverizes the baked soil. As a cold, steel downpour follows, driven oblique by the wind, it erases the landscape. The storm strips whole limbs from the desert willow, presses leaves mixed with trash to the fences, knocks men off their feet. Twenty minutes later it's over. The track is liquid sediment. Departing clouds leave a million reflected suns floating in sheets of water as drying begins. My cell smells like creosote, a fragrance so heavy it lies against my skin, saturates my clothing, draws down inside my lungs. The desert's tonic, mixed with rain, soothes heat-weary joints and marrow.

Heavy thunderstorms that batter separate regions characterize the monsoon season. Just as spectacular are the results. The desert greens again. Grasses resprout, ocotillo and creosote releaf, barrel cacti flower. Desert marigold and sometimes brittlebush take this wet opportunity to bloom again. Mesquite trees, too, start a second crop of sweet pods. The summer annuals, wildflowers like devil's claw and summer poppy that skip spring and wait for warmer and wetter days, suddenly appear. Cacti fill their storage-jar stems. Sonoran desert toads and spadefoots break their fasts and search for mates while frenzied harvester ants rise in nuptial clouds. There is an urgency to take advantage of the season. It is a second spring.

Monsoon weather continues with its regimen until mid-September or so when the tropical winds retreat and the desert gradually dries out again. Under clear skies and shrunken humidities mesquite pods ripen, hanging in blond clusters like my oldest daughter's French braids. Late bloomers, the barrel cacti, now ignite with sunburst garlands while the seed-plumes of desert broom collect in snowy drifts. With the stress and fervency of the last few months subsiding, the desert relaxes, exhales one long, slow breath. Aftersummer glory settles in. Bright, hot days grow short and balmy; nights cool. The incandescent heat lamp of summer dims to a forty-watt soft glow. Aftersummer days can be hot but nights are comfortable. Toward its end there is a pulse of activity: butterflies and grasshoppers hug the fences while resting from some exodus; hairy caterpillars race across the track with an urgency for leafy places to spin their cocoons; the swallows take off for Mexico.

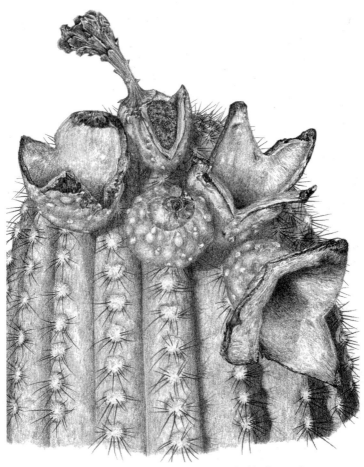

Fruiting Saguaro Cactus

Then, in one day, fall enters with the Pacific storms of November. If the cold weather holds, which is never certain (we could have three or four "falls"), the cottonwood canopies at the Rincon Unit, the largest trees on the complex, will turn golden before the leaves scatter altogether. It's as traditional as we get. Winter annuals germinate, their inconspicuous rosettes smudging the ground, and the reptiles begin their long sleep. Harvester ants won't forage when temperatures can't climb above 64 degrees.

January's few weeks of winter are an extension of fall. Pacific fronts continue to bring rain and, occasionally, snow. But alternate days are just as likely to be sunny and mild. Our only mesquite tree is bare, a fretwork of blackened and arthritic fingers reaching in the only direction to escape this confinement—upward. Cacti and paloverde still benefit from sunlight that drenches their evergreen branches. Creosote might even flower. It is an uncertain time. A sudden storm could bring frost or snow, or a few days of sun may feel like spring. But the desert's unpredictable nature isn't difficult if we're flexible, if we adjust to it. We might even begin to accept it.

I can. It's true that prison's gravity has punched a hole in the three-dimensional space of my life, narrowing it down to a single point, muddling my past, my future. That without distance I can't measure time. That I live in a kind of endless present. But here, in those quiet moments when the prison system is not too much of a distraction, when I'm not buffeted by meaningless or sadistic rules, I find clarity.

Prison, in itself, can teach me nothing of value. It only concentrates what I already know, who I already am. The desert cuts through more of the strata of my life than prison ever will. It touches layers much deeper than the simple limitation of bars and fences and cells. In this way the desert has influence. I respect it. It is my mentor. I learn from it how to adapt to adversity, not from those sorry pack rats that hole up in their insulated cells but from the lizards and snakes and tortoises, the wildflowers and brittlebushes and saguaros that push past vulnerability and overcome, even flourish.

One result of my struggle to learn from the desert and adapt to my circumstances, my prison environment, is an unshakable sense of hope. Even during the longest, driest, most skin-cracking, lip-blistering foresummer, the saguaro produces fruit. John Steinbeck says that hope warps the way we think about our world. Probably. Hope may be a product of denial whose purpose is to disguise reality, to lessen its shock or to escape it altogether. But for me, hope gives me the motivation to face my reality and patiently work my way through it. In this, hope becomes my jailor. Hope is a better security system than all the guards, electric locks, fences and concertina wire, motion detectors and infrared sensors put together. It's what keeps me going in prison, hope that a petition will be heard, that a new law will open the gates or, if I don't get some early relief, that I will make it through the years to my release—and beyond. I have become a disciple of wildflowers and brittlebushes. I am tortoise, saguaro. I will survive the seasons of heat and frost and storm, and I will survive this drought.

Fremont Cottonwood

Richard Shelton loans me his copy of *Trek! A Man Alone in the Wilderness* by Geoffrey Platts, a local guru of environmental causes, and when I turn to page ninety-two a single cottonwood leaf slips into my lap. It is a gift from the author, no doubt, although he could never have imagined the leaf would find its way into the hands of a prisoner. I'm appreciative, thrilled. There are no cottonwoods here, and it's been a long time since I've held one of these untreed tokens of rivers and summer.

There is a pain that arises whenever something reminds me of what I'm connected to. I risk the pain of memory by turning the leaf over in my hand, raising it to the light of my cell window, pressing it to my nose. Thin and brown and veined, it is an old vegetable hand with delicate lifelines of history, of youth's chlorophyll glory, of midlife's insect scars, of death's wrinkles and liverspots. I hold hands with the corpse of a familiar desert oasis—Sabino Canyon, Romero Pools, San Pedro River—and it speaks to me. Vegetable words. I open my notebook to embrace it, to preserve it in pencil, an act of compassion that loosens my thoughts to drift and settle among boulders slick with the mossy breath of black water, and risk, further, the blood of memory.

Silverleaf Oak

I can see the tonsured pate of Old Baldy from my cell window. The peak is always there, a fixture on the southern skyline, always dead serious. And not just from my narrow window. Mount Wrightson rears up from the wrinkled Santa Rita range and makes its presence felt—at least for me. I see it from everywhere in this prison. It follows me when I walk the yard, glares at me while I wait in line for my commissary. From beyond the fences it draws my attention like a lover I cannot attend to. Too much of me is tied to the place, and the mountain keeps testing the knots.

Madera Canyon scoops out the right side of Mount Wrightson and spills onto the desert. The canyon is a classic riparian drainage of cottonwoods, ash, and sycamore. Silver-leaf oak and alligator juniper pepper the dry hillsides, but in the deep grottoes, water seeps from banks held tight by horsetails, mosses, and yellow columbine and fills dark pools thick with horsehair worms and diving beetles. Pale gray tongues of lichen lick granite boulders unscoured by high water. The canyon is home to creatures with mysterious names: brown creeper, hermit thrush, wood pewee, elf owl, coatimundi, elegant trogon. It is a place where gnomes might still live in some of the old, hollow sycamores.

Under the cynosure of Old Baldy, Madera Canyon is both a beginning and an ending for me. It marks the first entry in my notebook after leaving prison. It is also the last entry, sixteen months later, before I came back. I notice now the paucity of notes I took on that first trip. The date was January 10, 1995, our fourteenth wedding anniversary, and I was distracted with other matters. Karen and I had a cabin for two nights. We were alone, together, for the first time in almost eight years.

We passed the days simply, hiking along the stream and birdwatching. The smell of juniper competed with moldering leaves. The crisp sound of our footfalls hung around our ears. The canyon breathed in our faces. I had rarely been so focused on details. I searched the hillsides for the perfect desert spoon to sketch and failed to capture the delicate pattern of a skeletonized cottonwood leaf. Winter's landscape mesmerized me. I could relax under the restrictions of my probation. "Like a prisoner sprung from a dungeon," Edward Hoagland writes after an operation restored his eyesight, "I didn't care about minor harassments, frictions, frettings, and inconveniences." Nothing inconvenient even existed for me. I had much more than fresh cornea implants. I had emerged from a chrysalis with a whole new set of untried sensory equipment. Karen found my childlike enthusiasm with my freedom amusing, but she was even more wondrous. Madera Canyon was her gift to me, and she included herself under the wrappings. In the evening we stretched out on blankets in front of a fire and fed each other roasted mushrooms and chunks of pineapple from sputtering shish kebabs, risking

Yellow Columbine

Desert Spoon

the tips of our fingers. I owned the acute pleasures of tasting the essentials—the wilderness and my wife.

Six seasons later the last entry in my notebook reveals more—lists of birds (including a new species for me, a male black-headed grosbeak), lists of plants, a description of the cabin, a description of the wooded ridge above the cabin where the oaks were beginning to recover from the driest spring in ninety years. I knew I was going back to prison in three days. My handwriting, thin and hurried, betrays some of my desperation. I wanted to write everything down. I wanted to freeze every moment in words because soon words would be all that I had.

This time, Karen and I brought our daughters. Our activities were becoming desperate, too. We explored the drought-deciduous oaks on the ridge twice, hunting for bear scat at Melissa's insistence. We collected pinyon cones, oak galls, tiles of moss, beards of lichen, shards of quartz. We scattered seeds for the birds and allowed a curious white-breasted nuthatch to charm us. My intention was to spend some time alone with each of my girls. I didn't have a plan, no rehearsed words. This wasn't goodbye. I knew my children would visit Madera Canyon again and again over the next four years of my absence, and I wanted them to have a few memories with me there until we could return again together. I was making desperate memories, shored up by the canyon and wild souvenirs from the mountain.

Evening. I'm drinking hot orange pekoe with a sprig of fresh mint that grows among the rosebushes in the inmate park. It's dark outside my window, but I can still feel the presence of Mount Wrightson out there. It shoves its way into my mind, and I wonder, feeling the melancholy, if it is a good thing. Nurturing emotional ties to the outside, to family and friends, is what we call doing hard time. Many men prefer to cut themselves off from their previous life and develop a tough layer of indifference to it. Relationships are threatening to the emotional shell. The pain and helplessness of watching them slip away as friends, children, wives go on with their lives can be severe. Better to end all relationships and get over them quickly. It will happen either way.

. Friends go first. Then girlfriends, wives, children. Two years is about all the time it takes. Parents, who generally feel some responsibility toward their sons, hang on, visiting on weekends and sending along some money. In prison, thirty-five-year-old men may get a monthly allowance from Mom and Dad. For families, I think death would be easier to accept and deal with than a son, dad, or husband in prison. Consider the demands of the long-term terminally ill and bed-ridden. Prison carries an enormous emotional burden that the whole family is sentenced to for at least as long as the inmate spends behind bars. Possibly longer. At least with death there is an end, and there are survivors.

Now, at the expense of my family who must share my incarceration of twelve years, I continue to make contact. Weekly visits, fifteen-minute phone calls, and letters aren't enough. These only begin to touch their world of rushed meals, inadequate budgets, neglected housework, jobs, homework, and pet concerns. Beyond these, I write my daughters' teachers and develop lesson plans for them. I record bedtime stories and play guitar for them on cassette tape. (I even recorded the answering machine voice.) Jessica and I share stories. We worked together on one about the summer she raised toads from tadpoles in her aquarium that *Reptile Hobbyist* published this year. Kasondra and I are caring for tropical fish, box turtles, a green iguana, and kittens. Melissa, now ten, and whose soul is poetry, trades metaphors with me. Despite prison, we win science fairs, become Student of the Month, publish artwork in *Highlights Magazine,* write poems to represent the school district—we enrich each other's life. Hard time is a good thing. Protective shells are for isolated embryos. Prison does narrow a life down to essences, and I find that I'm left clutching only what's most important, like relationships.

Often when Mount Wrightson draws my eyes above the southern perimeter, I think about the day I finally climbed its summit. Ten months out of prison, I was in my first semester at the University of Arizona working on my M.F.A. in creative writing. I was new to the program and uncomfortable with the peer group, but I wanted to fit in. When several graduate students invited me to join them on a Saturday hike up to the peak, I accepted. I knew I'd be in my element, on familiar ground. I could make friends.

I met Greg, Chris, David, and Matt at the "Old Baldy"

Gray-breasted Jay

trailhead at 9:00 AM. The sun had just pulled away from the upper ridges and broken light raked through the oaks. The only sounds were the approaching calls of half a dozen gray-breasted jays as they leap-frogged one tree at a time up the canyon.

I knew everyone except Greg from the course I was taking that fall semester. Before I joined the program I'd hiked with Chris and Matt. The previous spring, Richard Shelton and a coterie of his student poets had decided to celebrate

Sonoran Mud Turtle

the warm weather with a trip to Romero Pools and an afternoon swim. I tagged along, taking notes for a future article about the herptiles—amphibians and reptiles—of the desert oasis, to hide my nervousness. I suspected they knew I had recently gotten out of prison (Richard probably had mentioned it) and I was anxious about it, although willing to discuss it. I was more afraid that being locked up for eight years had made me socially inept. As it turned out, I wasn't entirely out of place with my soon-to-be classmates. While the group pondered the merits of postmodern poetry, I identified the local flora and fauna, some of which, such as a pool-probing Sonoran mud turtle, appeared on cue to ease my tension. I may not have understood the language of poets, but I did own the words of nature. We visited Romero Canyon twice that week, concluding the hikes with stopovers at Richard's home for juice coolers, a citrus concoction of his own invention to remedy parched throats and sunburn. It was standing in his kitchen that I suddenly felt I had joined part of an inner circle; even his dogs, Oso and Sadie, accepted me along with the others. I began to look forward to the graduate program.

Greg and I walked together up the steep trail toward Josephine Saddle. He talked easily about his youth work in Alaska, a background that was similar to mine with the Y.M.C.A. in Tucson. My words, in turn, came with the labor of the climb, short, clipped sentences as I grew increasingly breathless. I knew where the discussion of our pasts was leading—for me, directly into a lengthy gap that started after five years of teaching. When Greg asked how I came to the program, I told him I'd known Richard Shelton for a long time. "I'm a graduate of his prison creative writing workshop," I said.

I couldn't hide it, and I didn't want to. My friends all knew about my time in prison and the reason for it. They couldn't have been my friends otherwise since they wouldn't have had the choice to accept me for the person I am. Even in prison now my real friends know my crime. I've always been straight-forward about what I did, although the truth has cost me not only embarrassment, ridicule, and humiliation, but broken ribs and stitches. Rejection can be a serious thing in prison.

Greg had heard the whole story by the time we reached Bellows Spring. Chris and Matt and David were waiting for us there, and we refilled our two-liter soda bottles where cold water dribbled from the end of a pipe into a buried half-barrel. I lounged among the leafy columbine and Indian paintbrush and noticed ash, Gambel oak, and my first New Mexican locust since leaving the one that grew in the grass outside my cell. I needed the break. My legs were weak and shaking and my chest hurt from sucking air, the lack of which was making me dizzy. All those laps in prison hadn't helped with the gruelling uphill switchbacks. Too soon, we left the spring to a whitetail buck that seemed strangely unalarmed about our presence, and I remember wondering how alarmed Greg felt about me.

I recovered somewhat after we ate lunch at Bellows Saddle less than a mile from the summit. Quick energy food: bagels with cream cheese, Gardetto's Snack-ens, and a banana. Then, more switchbacks. The sun and climb warmed us out in the open above the trees. I peeled off layers of clothing with the rise in elevation—unusual. I had expected it to be cold at 8000 feet in the middle of October, but even the lizards were out enjoying the sun. The reptiles also seemed unaffected by us, only eyeing us from their lichen-encrusted perches, their emerald and malachite scales in chromatic competition with the green, yellow, and gray symbiotic plants.

Four hours from the parking lot we signed the register at the old fire lookout foundation on top of Mount Wrightson. The peak was rocky, windswept. Tufts of perennial grass and some bent and creeping shrubs, possibly skunkbush, furred the otherwise naked dome. Even the ladybugs stuck to the crevices. That afternoon, however, there was only a touch of breeze, just enough to apologize for the heat and allow squadrons of tiny yellow gnats to orbit our heads without a struggle.

We stood above the haze. In all directions its striations obscured the valleys. Distant mountain ranges buckled and then dissolved into the smog. The Catalinas were washed out, but Baboquivari Peak managed to drive its thumb above the

Alligator Juniper

flat, white horizon. I recognized the dark green slip of the Santa Cruz Valley to the southwest, and farther, where the landscape rippled, Mexico. But in all that panorama, a certain creosote-smudged basin in the north held my eyes—a topographic polygon of razored desert where time held its peace. It connected me by belly chain. I had thought that scaling Mount Wrightson with my new friends would be a personal milestone for me. And, I hoped, a conclusion. It wasn't. Something lingered: fears of an uncertain future, possibly. In my notebook I wrote: "How many times had I looked up from that prison yard and hoped to climb this peak? Now I can't help but look down at that place." The irony of fate. Was it only my fears or did I really imagine I had a few more years to covet Mount Wrightson from behind fences?

Although I was miles removed from the place, prison still gripped me by the wrists. Then, I couldn't avoid the physical restraints imposed on me there. Now, I couldn't avoid the emotional restraints noticeable on the peak. I wasn't entirely free. Prison followed me. It *was* a life sentence, I realized, and it had imprinted on me at some deep level. Furthermore, I began to understand that simply because I had walked through those gates I wasn't necessarily free from doing hard time. Hard time doesn't depend solely on prison; it depends on relationships. Prison only concentrates and enhances the inevitable pain all relationships cause (and prolongs this pain because prison, at its best, suspends rather than heals), the pain (or grief) of separation, failure, broken promises, broken trust. In or out of prison I could do hard time—and anyone else who cared about me. Hard time by association.

I next saw Greg at the start of spring semester. We were taking Vivian Gornick's nonfiction workshop together and working on the *Sonora Review.* He was one of the poetry editors; I had recently accepted the position of nonfiction editor beginning with the next issue, number 32. The semester was tenuous for me, but it was also a gift, time on loan. The day after Thanksgiving I learned that the appellate court had overturned my judge's decision to release me. The state was determined to send me back to prison. My freedom now depended on the Arizona State Supreme Court and its favorable ruling.

In the first week of July the court decided not to make a decision, allowing the appellate court ruling to stand. I had less than two weeks. I met with the other editors at the *Sonora Review* and told them the news. No one could believe it. I couldn't believe it. Greg was stunned. Before I left, we spoke together in one of the offices. He said it was the worst thing he had ever heard, and he intended to write some letters for me. Then he hugged me. His compassion, the kind that arises from a powerlessness to do anything else but empathize, ripped me apart. We could have been good friends.

Months later, back in his prison writing workshop, Richard Shelton told me that the editors had dedicated *Sonora Review* #32 to me.

>—◆—○—◆—<

On my bulletin board in my cell are photographs of friends and family: me in the center of an arc of men from my church; Karen holding a kitten and smiling; Jessica, Kasondra, and Melissa in their Easter dresses; Karen and me sitting on a stone bench in Bisbee; the girls and me in the front yard; the girls and me in the mountains.

The bulletin board is a kind of shrine, each image my own sentimental notion of relationship, of love, reduced to a three-by-five snapshot. Where prison itself fails, it reminds me of the magnitude of my crime, the lives affected by it ... affected by me.

Great Horned Owl

RAPTORS AND FLYCATCHERS

At 10 PM on the eve of *el Día de los Muertos,* the Day of the Dead, a great horned owl materializes at the end of the run. At first I think someone has left a mop leaning against the railing, but then the mop head shifts slightly and a pair of unblinking yellow eyes focuses on me. The bird is huge, out of place. It *should* be a mop head. The yard is on lockdown and the run is dark. Most of the cells I can see from my window are dark, too. The owl perches twenty-five feet away, right outside the last cell on the upper tier.

I wonder about the significance of this oddity. Only once have I seen a great horned owl at the prison. It appeared at the fenceline, a creature of the edges. It was a glimpse at the periphery of my vision; now it's a ghost at the periphery of my mind as I begin to doubt the memory. This one is undoubtedly interested in balancing out our over-population of mice, but its presence is still too bizarre, surreal, a wild predator among all this moon-blanched concrete and steel. "An owl of the waste places," as the Psalmist says. Even the human predators don't come out at night here. But I can't doubt my eyes. And there's no mistaking *its* eyes. I wonder if that stare can see inside me to the awe and pleasure that stirs there.

Manny, one of my Navajo friends, has told me that his people believe owls are something to fear. "It's a bad omen to see one. They carry off the spirits of men, and shamans use them for evil." I asked him if it was true that when an owl appears outside your house, it means you'll be dead by morning. He said he didn't want to talk about it anymore. Now, I decide not to mention to him that a great horned owl had stood directly above his cell the night before the Day of the Dead.

The owl bobs its head and half-unfurls its wings. In an instant it is gone. I'm not sure it flew. It just sort of jumped suddenly and vanished. I blink my eyes and feel cold air leak in from under the door. The owl has restored my faith in things wild, supernatural.

We have other raptors that occasionally visit the prison: red-tailed hawks, Cooper's and sharp-shinned hawks, kestrels and burrowing owls. Twice I've watched golden eagles spread their huge Pleistocene wings over me. A few years ago a redtail killed a raven as it picked through one of the garbage dumpsters just outside the perimeter fence. Squalid and undignified birds those ravens, ever-present, ever-numerous (I've counted fifty together in one flock), always prowling the area for handouts or scraps. Some native peoples revere the raven as a mythic figure, a trickster like the coyote. Richard Nelson, writing about the Koyukon of southeastern Alaska, says the raven is seen as "good and evil, sage and fool, benefactor and thief—the embodiment of human paradox." But to me the oil-slick birds embody the essence of this place; they are scavengers of landfills, human or otherwise.

The scene attracted quite a crowd. A couple dozen men lined up along the fence to study the hawk as it casually pulled breast feathers from its victim, the black plumes para-chuting on the air like ashes drifting away from a trash fire. For forty-five minutes we watched the redtail stuff its crop with long, red elastic ribbons of flesh pulled one after another from the raven's body. When the hawk finally flew off to settle on a light pole, strop its beak, and preen, it left behind an eruption of feathers, some peeled bones, a pair of feet and a beak. The remnants, splayed and twisted there atop the dumpster, reminded me of those finely detailed fossil impressions of archaeopterix. But archaeopterix may have had more meat on its bones.

The men here still talk about that base act of nature. That redtail made an impact on more than the raven. There are those who believe that biophilia, the word E.O. Wilson coined to describe our "urge to affiliate with other species," is in our genes, something inherent from our human cultural beginnings. We are a species prone to worship creation rather than the creator. But, I think, as is the case of other gifts we are born with, that bond must be nurtured or it withers. It's encouraging for me to see the men stop and take notice of wildness. It demonstrates their humanity, their connection to nature as an integral and essential part of life. This connection to nature may even be more essential than freedom. The worst kind of punishment forbids any form of contact with another living thing: solitary confinement, the "hole," a concrete cell without windows, without crickets and cockroaches. But imprison a man with trees and he will sit under them, with insects and toads and squirrels and he will make pets of them, with swallows and he will count them.

A fence is not a barrier to my expressing my innate need to love life. But the mind can be. If I walk laps around our half-mile exercise track with every step clouded with thoughts of what I'm missing being away from my family, I withdraw from life. The walls grow thicker, the fences higher. And, ironically, my family becomes more distant with the years remaining until I again join my wife and children stretching out between us. I won't even see the weeds blooming at my feet.

Lately, a sharp-shinned hawk, the smallest of the bird-hunting clan that also includes Cooper's and goshawks, has been frequenting the prison to dine on bread-fattened songbirds. (It's illegal to feed the birds, but some of us can't help this criminal behavior.) Sharpies are crow-sized with short wings and long tails, the classic accipiter design for speed and maneuverability. Adults show a reddish cross-barring on the breast, but according to the descriptions I'm getting, the one on the yard is a juvenile—brown streaks its breast.

I haven't spotted the sharpshin yet. Two friends told me it had entertained them yesterday during a lockdown by deboning a house sparrow on the lawn outside their cell. Better than television, they said. Biophilia again, and they enjoyed telling me about it, this real-time predator ritual that touched them with the morality of wildness, with the flow of energy from those eaten to those who are the eaters. Primal stuff. We reminisced about the redtail/raven vignette, and I asked them to let me know if they see the hawk again.

A sharp-shinned hawk would be new for me, one more bird to add to my prison "life list." It would definitely be a rare find for this place in the same category with the immature Cooper's hawk, sighted once several years ago, the twice-seen golden eagles, and that recent, still-mystical great horned owl. Seeing a sharpy in prison would, for me, be on the same level as seeing an elegant trogon in the Chiricahua Mountains, or a Mexican gray hawk on the San Pedro River.

Red-tailed Hawk

For the past week I've been alert for the sharpshin, checking off each pole, fenceline, and housing unit during my exercise walks on the track. Today, I'm expectant. It's going to be a fine birding day. Already, before I can get started, I hear the plaintive call of a flycatcher, an uncommon bird at the prison in November. The descending cry penetrates the walls of my cell from a distance. It instantly catches my ear, even above all the distracting and perpetual white noise of televisions, paging systems, heating units, flushing toilets, and chattering voices.

After the noon lockdown and count, the prison yard opens again and I head toward the call. *Pee-ur, pee-ur,* the bird cries in a minor key, delicate as breath. *Pee-ur, pee-ur.* At the first bend in the track I locate the source of the sound. The flycatcher turns out to be a pair of fledgling Say's phoebes, perched side by side on a spring of razor wire. I stop to watch them. *Pee-ur, pee-ur,* one of the birds whistles. In seconds a parent arrives, cutting a sharp path across our artificial wetland to the begging chicks. Where is the nest? I wonder. And why this time of year? It seems terribly late to be raising a brood.

The parent phoebe strokes back to the wetland and skips for insects in the mangy, yellowing grass. There seems to be no lack of prey. I will encounter this family of flycatchers over the next few weeks, always hearing their wistful and distant song before sighting them. In two days only one chick will call, stationing itself more often than not on a stake in the center of the fallow wetland, and I will think there can be no better metaphor for loneliness.

Later, walking along the fenceline of the visitation park, I hear something unfamiliar in the trees. The sound is a new configuration to my ears, a sharp *cheet, cheet,* and it's disembodied. I can't find the bird, if it is a bird and not some clever insect, among all the gray, mottled branches and dark leaves. I wait. When it finally sallies out to crack open a beetle I've dislodged from somewhere, I recognize it as another flycatcher, but I can't guess which one. I make a mental note of its likeness—small, gray on back, white on breast, fleshtone lower beak—so I can look it up after my walk. On one thing I'm certain—I haven't seen it before now.

Birdwatching in prison gives me reason to leave my cell. There's always the possibility of a new flycatcher to draw my mind away from the heavy aspect of this place and connect me to something untamed by these fences. If not a flycatcher, then a new hawk or owl … or even a new behavior from an everyday bird. While walking my circular course, I may not expect much, but I keep my mouth shut and listen more. I watch more. And whenever I catch a flash of wings, see an unfamiliar profile, or hear a warble, my senses narrow down to a point. I don't just see or hear but *notice*. When a flycatcher cracks open a beetle I'm involved. I've decided it's more important, this embrace with nature, than even my freedom. What's freedom without participating in life?

In the evening I complete my daily routine: ten laps, five miles. I don't notice the sharp-shinned hawk, but I'm not discouraged. I have time. I have many more miles. (One year I walked more than 1500, imagining I was unwinding every one of those 3000-plus laps and hiking cross country. Whenever the wind curled through the needles of the Japanese black pines in the administration area, I could almost transport myself onto a forested spine of the Rocky Mountains.) For now, I'll hold onto whatever grace sends my way: today, if not a sharp-shinned hawk, then a flock of red-breasted house finches strung along the perimeter fence like Christmas lights, or the lonely cry of a young phoebe seemingly as homesick as I am, or something entirely new, like a never-before-seen gray flycatcher, its secretive, half-whispered *cheet* held in my mind.

Soaptree Yucca

Nature is not always so aesthetic as those socially conscious, nature-as-art Victorian writers would have us believe—unless you consider, for example, that death by slow evisceration is a beautiful thing. I've often thought that if you want to write best-selling horror novels, you should first study the insect world. Lots of material there: the exploding harpoon mouth-parts of dragonfly larvae, the flesh-burrowing tendencies of bot fly maggots, the pit-trapping, sucking-the-dissolved-body-contents table manners of ant lions, or, something I've been seeing lately, the notorious lifecycle of the tachina fly.

There's a migration of inches taking place across the dirt track where I walk. Hairy black caterpillars are on a fall march, driven by some internal design to leave the relative safety of sap-thickening trees, drop to open ground, and run a gauntlet of shoes, tires, and beaks. It's insane, I think, this design. The larvae are too conspicuous, too edible. Maybe they taste bad. Or maybe their hairiness protects them. I've heard that some fuzzy caterpillars have irritating, stinging hairs.

Later, I scoot one into a jar and take it to the classrooms. We have microscopes there, and I want to examine this idea.

At four hundred times normal size, a single hair looks like the spiked shaft of a yucca stalk. Not barbs, but forward-pointing spikes. A granular substance speckles its length. Poison? If it's not venomous, it's certainly fearsome. I wouldn't want to brush these prickles into an eye.

Another caterpillar I collected two weeks ago had spun a cocoon, shedding its own hair and mixing it with silk. The oval bag was thin and I could see the dark shape of the caterpillar inside. I'm thinking now that the caterpillar is the larva of a virgin tiger moth, an ornate, black-and-white patterned insect that I sometimes see resting on buildings here with its wings raised over it like a tent. The caterpillars, called woolly bears, are known to spin cocoons mixed with their own hair.

Five days later the cocoon, still attached to a leaf in the jar, disgorged a small brown pill. I recognized it as the pupa of a fly, but I wasn't sure why it was in the jar. Now I have an answer. A large dark fly, resembling an ordinary housefly, has uncapped the pupa and emerged. I check out an insect key from the library and the book tells me it's a tachina fly, a member of the second largest group of flies—all predators—numbering more than 1300 species. Adults feed on flower nectar, but the immature tachina eats a wholly different fare. When she's ready to reproduce, the female lays her eggs or larva directly on the caterpillars of moths and butterflies. The fly maggots then bore into this living larder and feed on its tissues, apparently avoiding all the vital organs until the caterpillar develops and spins its cocoon. Instead of a moth or butterfly, flies hatch.

My caterpillar was nourishment enough for three flies. Beautiful stuff.

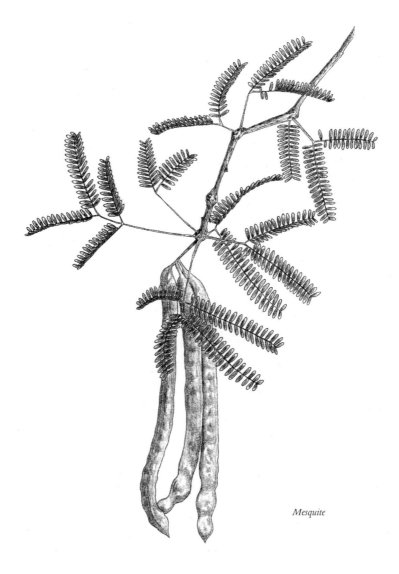

Mesquite

There is a fine connection between perception and emotion, what is sensed and what is felt. Feelings are susceptible to environmental influences of all kinds. Prison can work catastrophic changes and bring your mind to its knees. Eight years of wading through this place of desperation and bitterness has certainly strained my emotions into unrecognizable patterns of expression. This may be a good thing. My old way of dealing with emotion sloughs away like dead skin, manna from heaven for the dust mites, and new ways begin to form, coalesce, clarify. The mind is shaken, whipped, then centrifuged. I notice things on a more profound level. I spend a few hours under a tree or in my cell with pen and paper and I begin to write words that come from deep inside myself. Sometimes I will dredge up material from some oceanic layer rich in organic sediment, lost ideas that hold an emotional ancientness as if they had pooled up from my genes rather than emerged from my mind. I don't recognize them as my own or credit them as first generation. Yet I can't help but give them substance, to speak them, to write them down, and to share them with others, impressing myself if no one else.

I sit beneath the only mesquite tree on the prison yard. I know it well. I've watched it grow from a few badly pruned sticks into a humid, bug-clicking canopy, its trunk furrowed by memories of wind and sun, its limbs darkening and thickening like the arms of a weight lifter. By all appearances, mesquite is a brutal tree, its wrought-iron branches hard and crooked and armed with thorns. Its pinnate leaves are featherlike only to the degree that the raised hackles of a hawk are featherlike. It is my kind of tree: obstinate, rebellious, short tempered—characteristics of even the trees thriving outside this place.

Mesquite is tough, a survivor. Its tenacity has made it the scourge of ranchers who prefer a tamed rangeland. When hacked or burned to the ground it resprouts as a wicked thornbush. It resists pruning by growing more dense. Even poison doesn't always kill it. The tree does well in poor, rocky soils because it makes its own nutrients by harboring nitrogen-fixing bacteria. Its roots may dig to a depth of 150 feet to find water. And, mesquite is spreading. As much as ranchers try to eradicate it, their cattle scatter the tree's hard, indigestible seeds across country. Yes, I can identify with mesquite. It stands for everything that takes advantage of difficult circumstances.

In a few more months, this tree will releaf and then the first crop of mesquite fruits will begin to ripen, the pods hanging in clusters like blond dreadlocks and pulling on the branches, making them seem weary, sun-wilted. Unlike other legumes, mesquite pods don't split open. The seeds remain within the edible pods rich in carbohydrates and protein. The pods are pleasantly sweet and have the flavor of field-dried alfalfa. The taste always jerks my mind to past summers with Karen and our daughters when we would gather mesquite beans to roast and grind and sift with whole wheat flour and then bake into mesquite bread just for fun. The connection is nearly as acute as on the evenings when I smell mesquite smoke curling away from the Indian sweat lodge and I'm reminded of desert camping trips with my family.

I have never had such emotional connections with certain tastes and smells as during this time in prison. The scent of my wife's Lady Stetson or newly washed hair, the sweetness of a blade of grass between my teeth, the tonic of creosote and dust in the air before a storm—all have an affect on me. Food, also, seems to be a primary source of connection—but not the bland, starch-laden, vitamin-and-mineral-leached "chow" served by assembly line in our overcrowded dining areas. The food that touches me emotionally comes from home.

This time of year the Arizona Department of Corrections allows our families to send us seventy-five pounds of food—cookies, breads, pies (no fruit), ham, turkey, roast beef—from a pre-approved list. For three or four weeks around Christmas the lines at the chowhalls shrink and marvelous odors (for a change) seep through the ventilation systems among the cells. Everyone shares. The best tamale I ever ate I got in prison, a gift from a neighbor I hardly knew. Every year my mother sends homemade vegetable soup, and every year while it simmers in my hot pot my cell becomes her kitchen with its hanging copper pans, butcher block, spice jars, and drifting sunlight. Without her spiced tea, it wouldn't be Christmas, winter without pine in the fireplace. Karen's specialty is zucchini bread, and it tastes of our backyard garden, the two of us twisting the last of the giant neglected fruits from lop-leafed plants. This year my daughters made a pizza for me, its odd shape and toppings a product of their lively fingers and imaginations. I warmed it with my reading lamp and remembered all the "pizza nights" we enjoyed together during my temporary release. The connection was as poignant as the one that braces me whenever I look at that can of black olives Karen always includes in my package and see the clever faces of my children as they wave at me with olive-decorated fingertips. Karen knows all about my emotional hang-ups with food.

This December will be the last time we will have Christmas food packages from home. The department has won a costly and bitterly fought battle in the federal courts to end this politically unfavorable prisoner holiday tradition. There are just too many of us and the manpower is needed elsewhere. The guards should be checking for holes in fences rather than poking holes in tamales. Security, of course, is an issue, too. I tell myself I understand this reasoning. It can't be as spiteful as I want to believe. How could they understand the way food from mothers, wives, and children affects us? Affects me? Why should they care?

The mesquite shies away from a gray building that has been the reason for its loss of limbs on one side. It is illegal for any tree to provide a way of escape. Most trees here grow in oblique directions or in twisted, wasted configurations. Despite that the mesquite slips askew, it is surprisingly robust. Even in winter, its branches keep their leaves.

I know that during my temporary release from prison I was incapable of depression. All I needed to do was step outside, sit in the sun, water the garden. The exultation of life

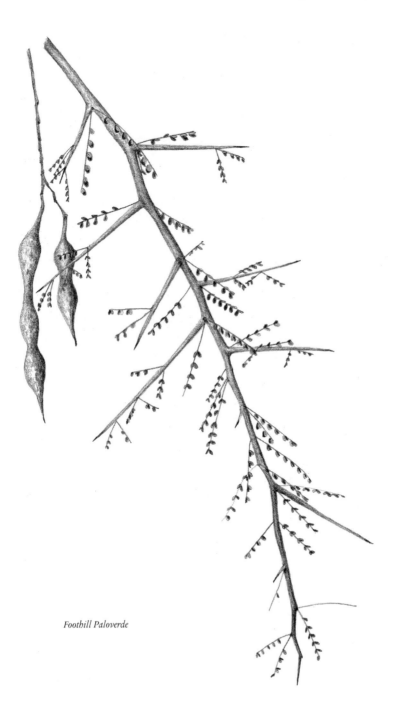

Foothill Paloverde

enclosed me, its sounds and scents. I was never so aware of the desert: flowers known previously only by drawings and names (desert chicory, larkspur, globemallow) that my children would carry to me as gifts; the fragrance of breath-moistened creosote in my cupped hands; the liquid trill of a canyon wren among the grottoes of Romero Pools—all this was so familiar to me, and more, although for eight years my experiences only amounted to words and pictures. I discovered that the desert won't let you forget, that it's always waiting for you to return, to be released.

Our first expedition as a whole family took us to the home of my youth to visit my mother. We never got to the front door. Instead, I gave my daughters a tour of the desert surrounding the house, a desert they had seen many times before but not through my eyes. The brittlebushes were thick and newly green and rubbed against our legs, marking us with scent. Foothill paloverde twigs caught in our hair. We had no itinerary, no purpose, except to allow grace an opportunity. Pack rat nests became a diversion; when Melissa found a sun-stained vial it became an observation glass for a scorpion. The desert had erased paths in my absence, but we visited my favorite places: an abandoned horse corral in brittlebush succession and an old, neglected, but venerable mesquite tree.

As a child I would spend hours in that tree, clinging to the rough branches like the emerging cicadas I first discovered there. I loved the rich coffee smell of the bark, the way it crumbled between my fingers and stained my hands. The earth beneath me was a mattress stuffed with the humus of tiny leaflets on which I could jump or fall or dive. Now, the mesquite's drooping branches enclosed it like the arching framework of an Indian hogan. Inside, a wiry cane cholla hugged its multiple trunks and thin bursage carpeted its floor. My girls were thrilled. They, too, saw the potential of this retreat.

For several weekends afterward we worked with the mesquite. First, we relocated the cholla and cleared away the bursage from under the canopy. We turned and smoothed the black humus with rakes and hoes until a fine powder like mushroom spores spotted the damp skin of our legs. Then, while the girls trimmed a few stems to widen an already natural doorway, I carefully started removing dead and weakened limbs, cutting them back all the way to the main body of the tree. There weren't many. Beetles had bored into a few; others had lost a competition for sunlight and became long, suckerlike whips; one had been sapped by a birdcage of mistletoe.

There is a difference between pruning a tree for its own good, following its natural form and inclinations and preserving some aesthetics at the same time, and pruning a tree with no more purpose in mind than improving security. Obviously. The same holds for correcting people. It is the difference between discipline and punishment: one looks forward and works toward restoration and health; the other looks backward and tears down, dehumanizes, destroys. It's ironic how prison treats its plants and inmates in the same way. Those top-cropped, emasculated ocotillo that stand at the entrance to this place imply more than an ignorance of landscape gardening. Pruning can enhance life, make it productive. Or it can be mindless butchery. There, at the mesquite tree near my childhood home, I was teaching my children to be neither mindless nor butchers.

I sit under a mesquite that is to me, among other things, a memorial to the desert that once defined this landscape. (Even in prison, I need a strong physical connection to place.) Despite the buildings that confine it, the concrete slabs beneath it, the mesquite will emerge from the barrenness of winter, the dead wickerwork of its branches flushing with leaves and slender catkins, growing heavy with pods. Bees will relay pollen messages to and from other mesquite trees outside the fences. Ground squirrels will cart away and plant its seeds. Like me, it is alone but not isolated. The mesquite may seem obstinate and rebellious in this way, as life itself is. But just as it doesn't really challenge the desert, it doesn't necessarily challenge the prison. It makes the best of it.

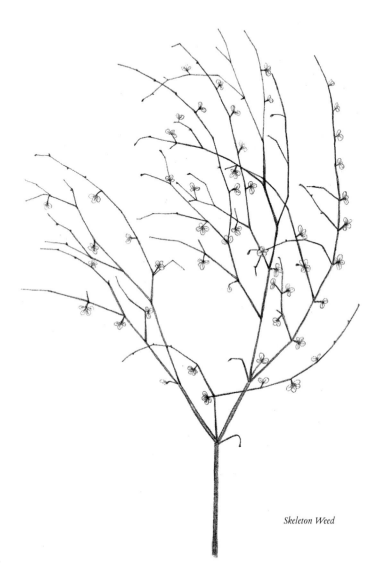

Skeleton Weed

Walking is an escape that frees my mind. While I am walking, the mass of fibrous roots that is my brain loosens and draws a few nerve-bound ideas to the surface. Today, on a cold December afternoon with Alaska sliding into the Southwest like a glacier and the wind polishing my teeth with grit, I think about elemental things. My body, like the planet, is mostly water, 98 percent or so on a good day. But water is an ephemeral thing in the desert, a gift with strings or, more precisely, a loan. You can't keep it for long; soon it evaporates or transpires or you excrete it as waste. When it's gone, when it's vapor, all that remains are splintering, crumbling tissues. A residue. Dust. Calcium dust. Phosphorous dust. Magnesium and iron and carbon dust. I am a collective body of mineral dust that wind once lifted and swept from dune to sky to dune, that once stung eyes and coated lips. When the wind comes, I taste the bones of those who were here before me.

I taste the bones of those who will follow me.

Filaree

In his book *The Island Within,* anthropologist and naturalist Richard Nelson writes: "What makes a place special is the way it buries itself inside the heart, not whether it's flat or rugged, rich or austere, wet or arid, gentle or harsh, warm or cold, wild or tame."

Of all the years I've lived in the desert, I've spent a third of them locked up. Yet it was in prison I came to understand that the desert is special to me. It touches me through these fences in the simplest and most profound ways. The unchained voices of owls and toads and coyotes, the trespasses of insects and birds and weeds. Someone once said that no one really loves the desert, but that the desert seduces you and takes you captive against your will. For me, it's a life sentence.

It is early February and already a little color competes with the winter-bleached Bermuda—in a few places anyway. Rising on slender necks above circular mats of dark, feathery leaves, lavender blooms of filaree greet a predawn sky. I notice them mostly before sunrise, before the blooms fade with the day. Today, on my way to work in the classroom, I probe

one plant with my fingers until I locate its base and then un-
thread it from the ground, roots and all. I will take it with
me, rinse its leaves and white, carrotlike taproot with water,
and turn the plant into questions.

Filaree is a wild geranium, a forb originally from Europe
but now naturalized in this country, particularly in the west
where ranchers appreciate its nutritional value for their cattle. It has other names—*Erodium, afilaria*—but most compli-
ment its long, slender, tapering fruits: heronsbill, cranesbill,
storksbill. When ripe and twisted into corkscrews, these have
an amazing ability to sow themselves, drilling into the
ground (or into your socks) as the humidity vacillates. On the
prison yard, filaree begins darkening the ground in late winter, staking out disturbed, marginal areas around tree wells
and fence lines.

There's another prostrate weed growing here that was
once thought to remedy rattlesnake bites and, although some
unfortunate settlers must have learned the hard way that it
doesn't, its name—rattlesnake weed—remains. I find it year
round, its stems creeping over bare earth like spokes of a
rimless wheel, paired leaves, dark and poisonous, lying side
by side. Rattlesnake weed, also called spurge, is a euphorbia
and a relative of the colorful poinsettias. It's as close as this
place comes to Christmas decorations.

I see that the weeds are blooming. The flowers look like
minute white cups, but what appear to be petals are actually
some kind of appendages, four or five of them, that house
several single stamens and ovaries.

The weeds and their flowers seem so insignificant, but I
marvel at their tenacity. Regardless of the weight of cold or
heat, the plants hang on as green and succulent, roots min-

ing the caliche for minerals and gaining purchase, leaves unfolding quickly or slowly but incessantly. Rattlesnake weed is another colonizer of disturbed places, the epitome of plants, poison and all, for a prison yard. It should be diagnostic of scraped and trampled landscapes, always just ahead of the hoe and boot heel.

I wrench up a rattlesnake weed to complement the filaree for a classroom diversion. Two flowering plants—the first of spring and right under our feet. The men might even be impressed.

I think it's odd how teaching has followed me into prison. Not only do I prepare the same subjects and use the same lesson plans and materials that I developed for my eighth grade classes, but I sometimes teach the same students. So far I've met six of my former students. Two I've had in the classroom again, studying the same lessons they never grasped originally. I tell them it's Karma, that they'll keep coming back to me until they get it right. Then, more soberly, I ask them not to hold against me any discipline I may have meted out in the past.

It took me several months after I came to the Santa Rita Unit to approach teaching again. In fact, I probably would have resisted coming back to the classroom much longer had the threat of disciplinary sanctions not forced me to work. The same year my school district awarded me Teacher of the Year, I returned the honor by disgracing the profession, my coworkers. Teaching in prison would only underscore the shame I felt about my crime. And it did. Because I was a science teacher, my first project was to create a science curriculum. I wrote my former teaching colleagues for materials, which they sent me. Each time those packages arrived I felt the pain; heartache came in manila envelopes, in lessons and activities written in the hands of friends who were ashamed to know me, who learned to avoid mentioning my name.

Ten years later I'm teaching that same science program. I still feel the sadness of loss among its pages, among activities like the one prepared by a friend who no longer writes. It calculates the diameter of the sun using basic geometry and a meter stick. The activity is my memorial to him. The depression has eased somewhat, but I'm not certain I've grown callous yet. I know I have to fight against the way prison can turn remorse into bitterness over time, as punishment persists without purpose. Punishment for the sake of punishment. Rehabilitation is the greatest myth about prison. Reconciliation is nonexistent. There's only meaningless retribution that soon enough overwhelms the criminal act. In the mind of many offenders it's natural to eventually place all responsibility on the system. What difference will it make to feel sorry about your crime? You still have to do the time. Every day I must fight to blame only myself for being in prison.

If there is such a thing as predestination, then regardless of where my stupid choices have placed me, my lot fell to teaching. This seems curious to me. I consider myself to be shy and introverted, even reclusive; I'm easily absorbed in the nonhuman world of nature. I notice wild things like bird song and tiny flowers but can't recall someone's name two minutes after we're introduced. I converse with people in constipated half-sentences—when I can make conversation at all. I'm more comfortable with wilderness where I'm accepted and reassured, where I understand the rules and agree with them. I've suffered hypothermia while caught in a

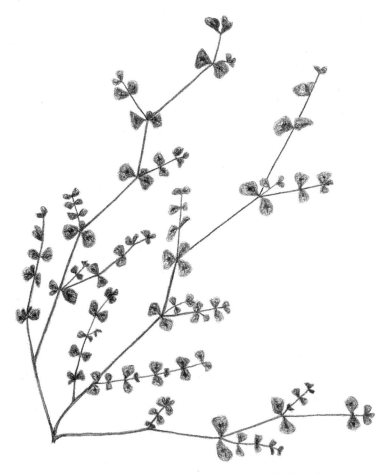

Rattlesnake Weed

mountain snowstorm. I've survived days in the desert without water, desperate with thirst. I've been trapped on cliff faces, lost in sunless crawlspaces while spelunking, stung by scorpions, bitten by spiders and snakes. But I've never been afraid, really afraid, until I came to prison. Only in prison have my fears become real. I've seen men die here, die from abuse, die from neglect. I know it could happen to me. The only broken bones I've ever had came after a gang assault while my back was turned. Nothing is more unpredictable and violent than human nature. Wilderness at its worst is never sadistic.

Yet, invariably, I'm shoved out of even my prison cell toward people. I organize events for our Christian Fellowship and lead song services at church. For seven hours a day, five days a week, I teach. Teaching certainly pushes the envelope of my personality, as most human contact does—except, possibly, the closest relationships of family.

I walk past cheeseweed, peppergrass, dandelion, and half a dozen other leafy invaders that I can't identify on my three-minute route to work. I will name them eventually. I can't help it. It's hard to resist this vocational inheritance from Adam, this innate compulsion to label things. I know that the act can distract me from enjoying the simple experience of wildness, that names can't truly describe the *scent* of creosote or the *flavor* of peppergrass, but the habit helps me order my world and communicate it to others, at least on a trivial level. I believe there is spirit in a name, particularly if the name is of common usage like rattlesnake weed, a name that speaks of character, true or false. Names make pathways in my mind for thinking, and without them I wonder if I could even think at all.

It's conceivable to me that I learn more by walking across this same plot of ground again and again than if I had the whole world to explore. Here, I miss nothing. The landscape is as familiar to me as my own body, the arrival of a new bird or plant on the yard as noticeable as the appearance of a new mole or wrinkle on my skin. Knowing place comes from knowing the details, being rooted through the seasons, standing still long enough to have some sense of it. In prison I notice things, not because they never change, but because they do.

When I can, I carry things to the classroom with me, found objects like raven feathers and fungi, a dead hawkmoth, sweet-tasting mesquite pods. Recently, I discovered a mummified bat in the gravel outside my cell. It was intact, posed, the dark paper of its wings and soft pelage of its body pulled up over its articulated bones as if to conceal its desiccated muscles and vacant organs. I dropped the animal into a plastic bag and brought it to the class, giving unspoken permission for the men to do the same with their own *objets trouvé*. Whenever they do, we have show-and-tell, passing around tarantulas on palms, toads in peanut butter jars, a whiptail lizard, a hummingbird corpse, the fallen nest of a flycatcher, the cocoon of a woolly bear caterpillar—each one a lesson plan.

I offer the students a taste of filaree root. No one accepts, and so I demonstrate that I'm not joking. The root should be bitter but isn't, tasting mild, radishlike. The men watch for my

Sacred Datura
"Jimsonweed"

response. I tell them that eating filaree root can settle stomach problems and relieve diarrhea. "Important information to remember," I add, "for your next bowel malfunction after eating those Italian sausages or chicken fried patty road kills." I go on to explain that the plants may be better than the medical treatment here. "You don't have to know twenty-four hours in advance of any impending injury or sickness and fill out the proper forms. Its dried leaves will help stop bleeding, and a tea made from them is a good wash for wounds and rashes. We should be drying the leaves and roots in our cells."

The men handle the plant. A few smell it. Then one asks if I've ever heard of jimsonweed. "It's supposed to grow here. Maybe you could bring it in?"

I laugh. I know what he wants. "Once in a while it pops up on the yard," I say. "But it doesn't stay long. Someone always pulls it up, and I don't think it's the cops."

Jimsonweed gets its name from a corruption of the words "Jamestown weed," so called because in 1676 the colonists of Jamestown, Virginia, used the plant to poison soldiers sent there to stop Bacon's Rebellion. The plant has quite a history—spanning thousands of years and many cultures—generally related to its mind-altering reputation. Some believe that Grecian priests burned jimsonweed at the Oracle of Delphi 2000 years ago. In ancient Europe and India holy men ate its seeds to induce prophetic visions; prostitutes slipped the seeds to their customers to enhance sexual excitement. In the Middle Ages jimsonweed was the poison of choice for those bent on murder. Native Americans used it for healing purposes or for religious ceremonies. It's hallucinogenic effects were particularly important for certain puberty rites among Southwestern tribes.

In the Southwest the plant is called sacred datura, which seems to me to be more descriptive than its other name, thornapple. (Its seed pods look like spiked globes.) The plant is holy to native people here. Its power comes from special alkaloids present in all parts—leaves, stems, roots, seeds—that alter the nervous system and cause symptoms ranging from nausea and dizziness to loss of muscle coordination, hallucinations, and, if not used properly, death. But the same chemicals also induce sleep, relieve motion sickness and pain, and treat hayfever, asthma, and some muscle spasms.

I tell the students that some people today aren't as interested in the plant's curing properties. "Years ago, someone was growing it in the greenhouse on this yard and getting high by eating its seeds or making tea from the leaves. Jimsonweed tea. But sacred datura is so much more than a source for a drug. It is a plant with a cultural heritage, once respected for its medicinal effects on the body *and* for the way it links the mind to the spiritual world—health to the body and spirit." I cut my tirade short before mentioning that I think our drug culture trivializes the real value of the plant. Most of the men I teach, I sometimes forget, are drug offenders.

Late afternoon I walk back to my cell. Overhead, a squawking flock of ravens outlines a thermal in black-feathered connect-the-dots, each bird in turn rising in spirals and boiling over the top. I step over other circular patterns, weedy fairy rings in the dead Bermuda. Over the years I've watched the rings expand, an underground growth of fertile soil traced at the surface by a lush green. There will be another lesson here this summer when monsoon storms soak the field and circles of toadstools raise their white, fleshy heads. Ringworm on a giant scale. More wilderness under our feet to warm my students' minds.

"I wonder," Richard Nelson writes, "what it would mean if each person, at some point in life, set aside time to become thoroughly engaged with a part of the home community: a backyard, a woodlot, a pond, a stretch of river, a hillside, a farm, a park, a creek, a county, a butte, a marsh, a length of seacoast, a ridge, an estuary, a cactus forest, an island. How would it affect the way each person views herself or himself in relationship to the natural surroundings, or to the earth as a whole?"

Nelson doesn't include prison in his list of home communities. But I wonder how many better places there are to set aside time to engage with nature. How many better places there are to allow nature to change some viewpoints, viewpoints like the significance of weeds, for instance.

Pinyon Pine

Gray is the color of cold at Santa Rita. Prison gray. A hard
wind gathers in wavering eddies, sifting plumes of gray sand
in one direction and then another. The hue suffuses everything, my clothing, my skin, my thoughts. It is a day for
holing up in my cell under blankets, sipping coffee, reading
books. At 7:30 AM I'm praying for a lockdown. It doesn't
come.

By evening my melancholy has not improved. I skip dinner and eat a peanut butter sandwich, triple-decker, instead,
washing the thickness from my throat with Folger's instant
and lukewarm tapwater. I should walk a few laps but the
weather won't cooperate. Exercise now would be a penitence.

On my bunk, I listen to the wind fingering the seams of
my cell and read Ed Abbey. Prison, with its chalky, blanched
stone, is an inorganic place, sullen, brooding. It isn't hard,
with the wind and stone and my gray mood, to imagine I'm
wintering in the canyonlands. Nature, in this place, and even
in the pages of a book, is not so much an escape from reality
but a penetration.

Sand creeps under my door like grain leaking from a
ruptured flour sack. The canyonlands: I scale a hill of sand

that creeps out of the high desert. It sucks at my boots, drawing me down slope, and I must take three times as many steps
to cover the distance. Behind me, sand slips away in sheets
like rolling liquid, gathering momentum and cascading
downward in miniature tsunamis.

On the other side a canyon dialates northward, bordered
by rising, uneven sandstone walls on the left and hills on the
right. Wind-pruned juniper and pinyon pine speckle the hills
and outline every naked dome and escarpment of protruding
rock. I'm standing at the broken feet of Hunts Mesa.

Farther up the canyon I hike along more alluvial terraces
beneath sun-glazed cliffs. Liver-colored minerals of desert
varnish percolate through the porous sandstone and stain the
orange walls in trickling liquid patterns. In places, whole sections of cliffs unscroll into narrow side canyons, potent with
color and shadow and the sexy shapes of water-worn stone.
In one of these I scuttle on hands and feet to gain a rim-
rocked alcove where vaults of rock span a slip of sky. I relax
in a natural cradle, mesmerized by walls that darken from
buff to burgundy with the ebbing sunlight.

My cell is dark beyond the glow of my reading lamp. The
air smells like dust, like canyon country, like wilderness. To
the eighteenth-century romantic, wilderness had to arouse
awe. William Cronon writes, "In the theories of Edmund
Burke, Immanuel Kant, William Gilpin, and others, sublime
landscapes were those rare places on earth where one had
more chance than elsewhere to glimpse the face of God." My
mood brightens. Along with being cold and windy and de-
pressing, this place also inspires me. Here, I have met with
God.

The Santa Rita Fire Brigade is our rapid response team trained to deal with medical, fire, and other forms of emergencies. It's made of men young and healthy enough to race to the firehouse, haul a large red wagon loaded with equipment across the yard, don heavy, bright yellow fire suits, helmets, masks, and air tanks, and drag coils of hose to any one of five hydrants. As silly as they look (spectators often supply the requisite siren noises whenever the brigade breaks out of its Tuffshed firehouse), the men have heart. They wear their blue T-shirts, silk-screened with the team's insignia over their chests, with a weight lifter's pride. We have inmate ambulance drivers at other prison units. Why not firemen at Santa Rita?

This morning, as I begin my exercise laps, Sergeant Basura* stands near some peppertrees in the park, hands resting at his hipless waist, dark head cocked upward on his thick neck. The man always has the same expression of contempt, I think, as if demeanor makes up for short stature. Now, he's turned it toward the trees. The fire brigade has launched the

---

* not his real name

wagon and a voice from the paging system orders inmates to exit the park area. There isn't a fire. I don't see a man down in the grass. But something concerns the sergeant. Something is violating policy, out of compliance, and I have an idea what it is.

I complete one circuit. Other men stop along the track to watch and I join them. "The peppertrees are blooming," I say to no one in particular.

"There's something in that tree," comes a response.

I laugh. "Yeah, Basura thinks he's found a swarm of killer bees and he's called the fire team to dispose of it. There is no swarm. Just lots of bees pollinating lots of flowers. I saw them earlier."

I was at Santa Rita when the Africanized honeybee scare arrived just prior to the actual bees. You would've thought the insects crossed the border into southern Arizona and targeted this prison with all the "swarm alarms." False alarms. And even when an occasional spill of honeybees coagulated among the branches of one of our trees, it was always a swarm of "killer" bees (what else could it be in this place?) and consequently destroyed.

Now, as I continue with my laps, I see that things haven't changed, except maybe the definition of "swarm." Two men in fire suits lift a hose and begin spraying the trees, first one tree and then another, sweeping each with a hard blast of white water. Sergeant Basura is gone; he's left the inmates to the task. He doesn't need to see the bees, dark and flightless, dropping to the ground like wilted blossoms.

Basura's been taking up space in my head lately, and as I walk I'm feeling the anger again. Several weeks ago he canceled my visit with my wife because he didn't like her attitude. Karen hates this place, hates the underside of human nature this place embodies, and doesn't hesitate to show it, to me, other inmates, the guards. Until my return to prison she was more tactful about expressing her feelings. But an attack on me at Meadows Unit quenched what little faith she had left and with it the will to be courteous. On this particular day one of the visitation officers brought me into visitation and immediately ordered me to the back office—a policy that infuriates my wife. The officer had not appreciated the way Karen had "tossed" her i.d. card and forms in her direction and walked away in silence.

"It has nothing to do with you, personally," I explained to her. "My wife is upset about being back here again." I told her how Karen had worked nearly eight years for my release and won it, only to lose our case on appeal and have another court send me back to prison after a year and a half of freedom. "I'll talk to her. There won't be a problem," I said.

Karen was waiting as the officer escorted me back to the visitation area. Her face was cold. "Does this have anything to do with me?" she asked as I pulled her away. The officer refused to acknowledge Karen's question, and Karen couldn't leave it alone. "This inmate here doesn't dictate what I do or say," she snapped. "If you have a problem with me, you will have to discuss it with me!"

Thirty minutes later, Sergeant Basura ordered me to report to him.

"Your wife is having a problem with *my* officers," he told me.

"There isn't any problem. I've talked to her and it's taken care of."

"No it's not. I'm terminating your visit."

I tried to explain that it would make things worse, that

he didn't need to push the issue, making much about nothing. But he was wielding his authority.

"I want to talk to your wife," he said, ending the discussion.

I have lost count of my laps, thinking about the ridiculous, pointless episode. What irritates me is Basura's insensitive treatment of my wife, his disrespect for her as a person. She's not an inmate, only married to one. His contempt for her is too similar to that of another Napoleonic sergeant who, years ago, ordered her strip-searched on an unfounded and malicious suspicion she was carrying drugs. With our three children present, Karen submitted to having a female officer examine her clothing, her body. The sergeant told her if she refused, he would deny her visits for six months to a year. A year later, Karen and my oldest daughter Jessica were still seeing a therapist. Jessica, six years old at the time, couldn't understand why people would hide things in their bodies.

Karen, by her own choice, hasn't been out to see me since she slammed the door to the sergeant's office and stormed past me. I called her to find out how she was doing. Basura told her she was a security risk and he would see to it that our visits were canceled permanently if her attitude didn't change.

Security risk? You have no idea, Karen had thought, looking around the office for objects to smash over his head.

"I'll have the deputy warden approve it," Basura said, and Karen knew he expected her to beg to keep our visits.

Without saying a word Karen reached for a scrap of paper and a pencil, intending to write down Basura's name and any other name he mentioned.

"Put that down!" he commanded.

At this point Karen began swearing at him and throwing paper, one sheet at a time, on the floor. "If you think you can threaten my husband into changing *my* attitude you had better think that over again. You're not terminating my visit," she said, finally, "I'm leaving!"

Karen hasn't been out to see me, but she has talked with Director Terry Stewart and met with the warden of the Tucson complex. She will see me again, and her attitude won't change. Like the rest of us, Basura will have to live with it.

To their credit, many officers aren't like Basura. Many aren't warped by power, just the ones, it seems, looking for promotion. Basura recently made lieutenant. I know I have a problem with sadistic cops, mostly because I also know they are unnecessary to maintain security. In fact, they do more to create problems with security. Karen was very close to losing control. She told me if one of our daughters hadn't been with us, the outcome may have been violent.

When I think about Basura, I see the faces of two other officers, a sergeant and a lieutenant (their names I never had the opportunity to write down), who had orchestrated the assault on me seven months before at Meadows Unit. Sadistic cops like to use inmates for their schemes, inciting us against each other. It's difficult to trace the cops' involvement back to them. Every incident is "gang related" or "racially motivated." I know guards who have leaked sensitive files of inmates they wanted harassed—even have made up "jackets" if the files weren't perverse enough. (One guard spread lies that a friend of mine was in prison for having sex with a dead body.)

I had put this kind of officer out of mind until my self-surrender last summer at Alhambra, A.D.C.'s placement and treatment unit. The court had ordered me to return to prison on July 19, 1996, and Karen and I had driven to the intake facility in Phoenix, parked outside, and walked in the front door. Waiting guards immediately escorted me away from my wife and the news journalists into a holding area to be stripped, searched, clothed in a bright orange jumpsuit, fingerprinted, and photographed. But my humanity didn't drop off with my clothes, with the loss of my identity and freedom. I guessed that something else must happen, something unrelated to incarceration. The inmates at Alhambra had serious problems, but the staff breathed contempt. It was a presence as much as an attitude. This is what I had forgotten. The inhumanity of the keeper. I never could understand how anyone could live like that, could choose a lifestyle of bitterness. What was it about prison that attracted this kind of person? One red-faced, toothless, obese sergeant at Alhambra only spoke in derisive overtones. I imagined him failing at his third marriage.

Alhambra is a fortresslike, red-brick structure of four wards enclosing an open courtyard—the "patio." Rows of narrow windows slot the exterior walls like gun ports; the inner walls are high and unobstructed except where a crop of radio antennas sprouts from the west end. Here, pigeons congregate around a plastic great horned owl, sometimes perching on its head. Some of the men fed the birds pieces of bread stolen from their meal trays and hidden in their socks. An act so incongruent with the place, like the rachet-voiced cactus wren outside my cell window, reminding me that the walls were not absolute but finite.

The first few days were the worst. Despair and loneliness pressed into my mind as twin parasites. I wanted to wail out loud, lying on a mattress on the floor, missing my wife, my children. I needed to see them, to hold them. Thinking about them was my only distraction besides sleep. There was little else. Alhambra was severely overcrowded. Cells, dorms, and day rooms all had men on the floor. Our days consisted of a routine of being herded to meals and an hour of "patio" in the courtyard followed by showers. My family occupied my thoughts, a painful obsession. Books, magazines, newspapers were contraband; cards and dominoes were confiscated. Fortunately, a friend I knew from Santa Rita had been transferred to Alhambra as a resident inmate worker. He became a resource for me. While my cell mates smuggled tobacco from other inmate workers, I smuggled books from Tony and read them over and over.

After two weeks the classification committee recommended I be reinstated as medium custody and returned to Santa Rita Unit. "We didn't know what to do with you," one of the counselors said, "which is why we've taken so long." I was less than three months from minimum custody status. Remaining at a higher security designation disappointed me, but at least the committee agreed to send me to Tucson. At Tucson I would be near my family. I could visit with my wife and daughters on weekends and phone them several times a week. At Tucson I had the support of family and friends.

About three weeks later, at three on a Thursday morning, the officers woke a large group of us, shackled us together in pairs, and loaded us onto buses. I was uneasy about our destination. Nothing was certain, and rumors were circulating about recommendations being meaningless. No one sitting near me seemed to have been classified for Tucson, but it relieved me to know the bus was heading south. Tucson is among the prisons in that part of the state.

When it was clear we were going to Florence, I hoped the prison city would be just a stop along the way. We drove past Central Unit and East Unit, two of the prisons that make up the huge Florence complex, and continued on to the Eyman complex, a facility that, like Florence, comprises multiple prison units. At Cook Unit a list of numbers was read and the men got off the bus. I relaxed. At Rynning, another list. Then, I heard my number. My chest caved in and my body trembled. I felt a strangeness cover me, a sudden cold, wet clamminess, and I wilted into my seat, dank and breathless. *What am I doing here?*

What followed were long waits in chain-link cages, uneaten sack meals, the exchange of my jumpsuit for new, stiff, oversized blue jeans, T-shirts, and boots. Depression wrapped around my confusion. *This wasn't supposed to happen. I'm too far from my family.* I felt sick, bloodless. When a guard told me I was going to Meadows Unit, another offered me details about its incompetent staff as way of introduction: "Meadows is what you get when you let these young guys who can't handle authority run things."

After hours in another cage, an officer finally gave me an inmate I.D. card and a plastic garbage bag of bedding and pointed me in the direction of my housing unit, a gray dormitory at the opposite side of the prison. Holding up my jeans with one hand, I dragged my bag across the pale, bare ground in the bright sun. The unit was quiet; only a few other inmates moved outside the dorms—controlled movement, I realized. High security. I couldn't believe this was a medium yard. It wasn't anything like Santa Rita—more fence, more razor wire, no movement without permission. The unit sank low in the landscape as if the desert had been gouged out from under it, an oval of steel netting with eight low dormitories laid out on the perimeter and facing toward the center. More fence divided the unit in half. Each dorm had four pods lettered A, B, C, and D and each pod twenty-eight bunks. When I stepped into my dorm, I noticed a guard in a cage who controlled access to the separate pods. I told him my assignment, 5-B, and the lock buzzed loudly until I pushed on the gate.

Eyes watched me walk to the back of the dorm to my bunk.

"What're you in for?" someone asked after I tossed the bag on my bed and began working the knot.

I turned around, then went back to the knot, ignoring the inmate. He was shirtless and his hair hung down his back.

"I said what are you in for?"

I pulled out my sheets, keeping my back to him. "It's a long story," I said.

The inmate persisted, "What are you in for?"

This wasn't Santa Rita. I had served nearly eight years of my twelve-year sentence there and had never been confronted about my crime. People asked occasionally, and I always told them, but it was never threatening. What I had actually done was more acceptable—less worthy of harassment, anyway—than what I had been convicted of. So I began to tell my story: "I was a teacher ten years ago. I got involved with a student ..."

"What are you in for?" he pronounced each word slowly. He wasn't interested in the details, and I suspected he already knew them. He had recognized me from the news.

"I ran away with a fourteen-year-old girl." I turned around.

"You ran away with a fourteen-year-old girl!" he repeated loudly, looking around.

I looked at him. I wanted to tell him that it was consentual, that we were in love, that I left my wife and children for her, that I was a fool. But he had heard all he wanted.

"You can't stay here," he said.

I turned back to my bunk and stuffed the sheets back into my bag. I walked to the officer in the cage and told him they didn't want me here. He opened the gate and told me to wait. A few minutes later he said the lieutenant at the yard office wanted to see me.

The lieutenant was young. His hair was straight and brown, cut short. He had a small, stiff mustache of the same color. He called me into his office and told me to sit down.

"Who's threatening you?" he asked.

"I don't know," I said. "It doesn't make any difference. I can't stay here. I'm too high profile for this place, and my life is in danger."

"So who's threatening you?"

"I don't know." I repeated. I had a problem.

"If you can't tell me who's threatening you, you'll have to go back to the yard."

He wanted me to inform on an inmate, and I knew if I did I wouldn't be safe on any yard. He knew it, too. "I can't," I said.

"You've got a sixty-one number. You know the system. But there's a policy now that says we don't have to offer protective custody to everyone who claims his life is in danger. Tell me who's threatening you, then I'll help you."

I spent another hour locked in the intake cage, waiting for another housing assignment. This time, they sent me to a dorm on the opposite side of the dividing fence. I stayed in 11-D twenty-four hours before another inmate questioned me about my crime. He listened to the whole story.

Friday evening, as I attempted to phone my wife, two officers handcuffed me and escorted me back to the intake cage. *What now?* I thought, sweating on the concrete floor. *Why don't they move me to Santa Rita?* After a while, a black officer walked past the cage, looked inside, and saw me lying there.

"Having some trouble?" he asked.

"Yeah," I said. "It's not good. Things aren't working out for me here."

The man paused, looking at me through the chain link. "I don't know if you believe in God, but prayer can help you." Then he turned and walked away. "I'll pray for you," he said over his shoulder.

With those few, simple words, the officer broke me emotionally. I thought he was the angel I'd been hoping for.

When the lieutenant showed up, he was with a tall, blond sergeant I hadn't seen the day before.

"What did you do?" the sergeant asked. "The inmates in your pod want to kill you."

His words hardly shocked me, but his tone made me instantly defensive. "You tell me," I said, "I was just making a phone call."

Then the lieutenant started: "You're talking about your crime."

"I've always told the truth about it. Do you want me to lie? I've been on the news."

"You're proud of it aren't you? Proud of being on TV."

"No, I'm not!"

"This is a medium yard," the lieutenant continued. "If you can't make it here, you won't anywhere."

"Send me to Santa Rita. I shouldn't be here. I never had any problems at Santa Rita."

"That's because it's 95 percent sex offenders."

"We're going to put you back on this yard," the sergeant said.

"Knowing they will kill me?"

"Who said they wanted to kill you?" the sergeant asked. "Maybe I was just f—— with you."

The sergeant unlocked the cage. "Come with me," he ordered. I was still in handcuffs, my hands behind my back, and he grabbed them and drove me to an office to look at a wall of inmates' pictures. He was impatient with me, angry. "Just point them out."

"I'm not a snitch," I said. "You want me to get killed?"

"It makes no difference to us. We'll put you back on the yard and then use you to strain spaghetti."

I couldn't believe what I was hearing. I began to fear the cops more than the inmates. The sergeant was threatening my life more than any inmate had. When he didn't get the information he wanted, he had me sign some paperwork that indicated my raised Institutional Risk Score. He then shackled both my arms and my legs. "You are now an I-5," he said. "You will speak only when spoken to. If you even turn your head and look at an officer, he will consider it a threat and take you down. Do you understand?"

I spent the weekend in the complex Central Detention Unit, solitary lockdown, without sheets, blankets, or toilet paper, sleeping on a bare mattress in my clothes and covering myself with a towel. Monday morning the sergeant in charge of C.D.U. told me I was going back to the yard. My third housing assignment was 5-C, one pod away from my first assignment.

Tuesday afternoon I dragged a new garbage bag of bedding across the yard at Meadows Unit. The officer in the cage accessed the gate to the pod and I walked the aisle to my bunk, dumped out my sheets and blankets, and began making my bed. As I leaned over to tuck in my blankets, the ceiling fell in on me. My head slammed against the far wall, ejecting my glasses and their lenses, and one quick pneumatic scream burst from my lungs. I couldn't take another breath. A staccato of fists and booted heels fell across the side of my head and ribcage. Something opened and my ears began to ring; something else collapsed and I lay still. As my attackers fled, I heard one of them yell, "You better get off the yard!"

Gasping with pain, I fumbled for my glasses and their lenses until I found them and made my way to the control cage. "I ... can't ... breathe," I said holding onto the wire.

"Wait here," a voice said.

I could hear the commotion around the cage. An inmate said that I had started the fight. An officer on his radio was requesting assistance. Other radios were squealing, officers with handcuffs, with video cameras. Someone asked how it happened. "I messed up," the officer in the cage admitted. "I let them into the pod."

More waiting. Lights in my face, a video camera, blood on my shirt. The gate opened. Someone led me outside and helped me into the bed of a pickup truck. At the medical unit more officers were moving around. A male nurse told me to lie back on an examination table. "I ... can't ... breathe," I said, sucking air in short, rapid gasps. Something had become disconnected in my chest and it snapped with each breath or movement.

"Focus on breathing," he said, "not on the pain." He pulled my shirt up to look at my ribs. Then pulled on my right ear. Liquid gushed down my neck. "You'll need some stitches there."

Someone wearing the white shirt of an administrator moved into the room and asked if I knew who had assaulted me. I said I never saw them coming.

"Why is it they never see anyone?" he said to someone else. Then to me: "See what happens when you don't cooperate with us? Maybe now we'll get your cooperation."

"I … didn't … see … them," I said, every word causing my ribs to pop in pain.

A guard took my glasses from my hand. Another threaded a belly chain around my waist and cuffed my hands into it. I yelled with each movement. "Focus on breathing, not the pain." When the ambulance arrived, they moved me to a gurney and wheeled me into it. A guard climbed into the back with me. An inmate was in the passenger seat. Another was driving.

At the hospital in Florence a technician wheeled me to radiology. Two officers watched as the tiny, middle-aged woman tried to maneuver me to get some pictures. I couldn't stand. I felt nauseated and the room began to dim. I was blacking out. She called the officers to help her get me to a wheelchair and asked if they would remove the shackles. "No ma'am. We can't do that," one of them said. She finally got me onto an examination table and adjusted her machine to take X-rays of my chest and head.

In another room, a doctor cleaned the wound behind my ear. It was messy, but not painful. "Did someone try to bite your ear off?" he asked, tugging on the lobe.

"I don't know. Why?" I asked.

"I can see all the way into your skull."

He stitched the tear and bandaged some other cuts. "You have two fractured ribs, but there's nothing we can do for them. I'll give you something for the pain."

Tuesday evening I was back at Central Detention Unit, strip-searched, and placed into a bare holding cage that smelled like stale tobacco and urine. An officer brought me a phone and I called my wife. She had already heard about me from the evening news. "I've talked to your lawyers," she said. "They're coming to see you. The deputy warden at Meadows told them the only reason you were in lockdown at c.d.u. was because there weren't any beds at Meadows."

"Karen," I said, "they tried to put me on that yard three times."

Late Friday morning, I waited in a cage to board a bus headed for Tucson complex. I learned later that one of my lawyers had driven to Florence that morning, but the deputy warden told him I had already been transferred to Santa Rita Unit.

It's been seven months since I arrived at Santa Rita. My broken ribs have healed. The wound behind my ear is now a scar hidden within a fold of skin. I still have a persistent ringing in my ears, but I only notice it when it's quiet, and it's not often quiet in prison. Emotionally, the incident has affected my wife much more than me. She no longer trusts anyone, and fear occupies her days. She's convinced the attack on me was planned within the prison administration, and she has reasons to think it was a conspiracy. Worst of all, Karen doesn't pray anymore. She has lost her faith in God.

I still have faith but not in conspiracies. There may be something to what Karen says, but I won't accept it. It's too frightening. Instead, I choose to believe what happened to me at Meadows was an accident, that I simply got caught up in a mindless, bureaucratic mechanism that treats people as numbers without concern for their welfare. Somehow, I fell between its gears.

I don't fault the inmates who beat me. They are only cowards, acting without reason according to the code, unwritten rules whereby a few inmates tell everyone else how to behave, as if our lives aren't ordered enough. I know there were three of them. I saw their pictures. The guard who worked the cage witnessed the assault, according to the department's internal investigator, who photographed my injuries at the hospital.

I do, however, blame that sergeant and lieutenant on swing shift at Meadows. They could have stopped the gears, but they oiled them. They violated their own rules of conduct. They disregarded their own humanity and compassion, even common sense. Regardless of who carried out the assault, they are responsible. They are the ones who have made the machine mindless.

⊢⊣⊷⊶⊙⊷⊶⊣⊢

The bees in the park still snarl in the peppertrees. They're impossible to discourage this time of year when there's new pollen and nectar to gather and restock last winter's shrinking larders. When the peppertrees are done, they'll move on to the desert willow as those come into bloom. Honeybees don't care about boundaries, whether fences or policies.

It may be unfair of me to place Sergeant Basura into the same category as the officers at Meadows Unit. Maybe I'm guilty of the same kind of stereotyping people apply to us. Criminals: they're all the same, all bad. But I'd like to think

I've given Basura the opportunity to operate this mechanism with compassion (or at the very least with indifference) to show he's human. Although my judgment counts as nothing. Either way, I can't allow him, and others like him, to occupy my mind for too long. I won't retaliate; anger is fruitless and only leads to bitterness. For my own health, I have to give them all up. It's the only way I can deal with this place.

I expect by now the incident and its records have become fiction. It wouldn't be the first time reports were lost or altered, particularly when lawsuits could threaten. My lawyers' requests for documents have gone unanswered. Karen says there's nothing in my department file that shows I was even *at* Meadows Unit. Writing about this now could cause me problems. A sobering thought. I'm in *their* prison, they like to remind me.

Honeybee

Brown Bat

Prison warns me to be unobtrusive and quiet, yet alert. I notice everything in this hostile landscape but choose to focus my attention, my thoughts and emotions, on the natural. (At least this is what I tell myself.) On this warm evening that smells of dust and cilantro, I find grace behind fences and razor wire with the coming of bats. Grace. And solitude, too. Western pipistrelles appear first, their tiny size and slow erratic flying making them instantly recognizable. Later, after dark, I should see some big brown bats and maybe a few Mexican freetails, but for now the tiniest of bats nourish my spirit, swooping and flitting as though reprieved from a life sentence. I imagine I hear the high mouth-clicks of their search-and-destroy radar as the bats hunt for flying insects. Or is it my imagination? There seems to be a ticking at the far edge of my hearing.

Occasionally, a western pipistrelle will spend the day attached to the education building where I work as a teacher's aide, the animal pressed onto the rough gray stucco like a splotch of mud on granite. Several times I've caught the bats by covering them with a plastic jug and then gently knocking them off their perch. They make wonderful impromptu science teachers, gracing us with lessons of form and function: the aerodynamics of elastic skin stretched between slender, elongated finger bones; the thermal regulation of capillary-webbed wings; the "vision" of ultrasonic chatter. Bats illustrate how finely tuned nature can be.

I know a man, Ron, who brought a bat into his cell after the mammal dropped out of the sky. He spent hours in the library thumbing through books on Southwestern wildlife to identify it and find out how to care for it. For a while it lived with him, spending the daylight hours in a "bat house" he glued together from pieces of cardboard. At night it flew around his cell, snagging moths and mosquitoes. Perhaps Ron couldn't convince his cell mate of the advantages of having a nocturnal insectivore (rather than a less efficient flyswatter) to deal with the bugs, for the bat soon disappeared through an open window.

A gray ball of fur the size of my thumb blows along the sidewalk gutter dragging a mouse's tail. It stops, then reverses itself as if the wind had shifted, but there is no wind. Another fur ball appears, this one a bit larger, and it drifts along the same route. Then, a third joins the pair. The gutter is a highway for mice, and it's rush hour.

Sometimes wildlife comes right up to your door, even when the door is made of steel, has electric locks, and leads to a cell. Today I've had more visits than usual. This morning Tony, my cell mate for the past few months, found a Great Plains toad in one of the shower stalls at the end of the run and brought it back with him in an empty peanut butter jar. He wanted me to release it in an area of grass and trees we call the inmate park where no one would bother it. Meanwhile, the toad didn't appreciate the tight quarters. While I got ready for my teaching job, it bounced repeatedly inside the plastic container, using all four legs in unison to raise itself only one or two inches in bursts of desperate energy. It wanted its freedom. I tucked it into my palm on the way out, an animated hiccup in my hand.

After dinner, Tony noticed another toad, this one outside the showers, pressed into a corner of the steps. It was too big for the peanut butter jar. Again, he wanted me to take it somewhere safe. This one was a large Sonoran desert toad, the two-handed variety if you plan on catching one. It clucked when I picked it up and its voice reverberated all the way down the run. Slime leaked from the bean-sized glands behind its eyes and long sticky strands webbed my fingers. Curious, I touched the tip of one finger to a gland and tasted the poison. It was bitter and numbed the surface of my tongue. Another inmate was watching me, and when I walked past him he said, "Hey, I've got a hot pot." I laughed, embarrassed. The toad hopped away under the chain link fence, out of reach.

Now, after lockdown, I watch the mice from the narrow, slotted window in my door and take notes. I wonder at their ability to tell time. At eight-thirty each evening they appear right outside, tiny, frenetic, adrenalin-crazed dust bunnies, rushing the seams of the sidewalk and around the concrete rock garden. When a guard approaches on the circuit to count the men, the mice ignore her. It's food they're after, leftover and discarded popcorn kernels, bread crumbs, fragments of a stale Fig Newton. The mice, two or three or four at a time, fan out and poke into every crack, every hole. They miss nothing.

Tony tells me he's concerned about the diseases the rodents might carry, diseases like the hantavirus that killed more than a dozen people a few years ago. I tell him that I think the virus was transmitted from the droppings of deer mice found in the Four Corners region of northern Arizona and New Mexico. These mice, I say, are house mice, *mus musculus*. No matter. He's heard the warnings. Warm-blooded mammals, viruses, rabies, sickness, and death. He says they should be trapped or poisoned. I think there are far worse dangers from two-legged animals, not only the men I live with but the ones in control of my life.

The mice are harmless, I'm sure. In fact, in the eight years I've spent in this place I've never known of a single life-threatening illness related to animals, despite all the scratches, bites, and stings. There was that day when a swarm of honeybees attacked half a dozen inmates and two guards. I'd heard a rumor that the bees were of the Africanized variety and had usurped one of the hives at the Santa Rita farm, a couple of fields of tomatoes and melons grown to supplement the starch we eat. There was also a teacher who teaches Pima College classes to inmates here who ended up with some nasty scratches on his hands and face after he tried to rescue a kitten stranded in one of the garbage dumpsters. Animal Control trapped eleven stray cats the next day before, finally catching the kitten. The worst animal-related incident occurred a couple years ago when a man was hospitalized after a small rattlesnake bit his hand. He said it had crawled through his window and struck him when he tried to remove it. More likely, the snake was a "pet" that bit him while he was showing it off.

Animal bites—and the resulting antibiotics, tetanus shots,

White-throated Woodrat

rabies vaccinations, antivenin treatments, and hospitaliza-
tions—are probably why the prison administration won't
allow us to keep pets, one reason anyway. It's too expensive.
But we do all the same. We break the rules. I wonder if it's
just another opportunity to resist authority or if it's related
to something deeper, some unconscious need for physical
contact with another living creature. Prison denies people
some of the most basic human gestures: the touch of a hand,
the embrace of a friend or lover. My wife calls the condition
"touch deprived" and recognizes it in me. Karen is aware that
the caress of another person releases hormones that blunt
anxiety, stress, and pain and cement emotional bonds. She
knows that touching clears the mind as well as it eases
tension, that there are profound psychological connections
between touch and love. But for her, this kind of intimate

contact needs privacy. We have "contact visits" without real contact. In prison every movement is watched, controlled. Policy even governs holding hands and kissing.

Chickasaw poet and novelist Linda Hogan says there are gestures reserved for animals because the distance between humans is often too great to bridge. "The hand," she writes in *Dwellings,* "is our contact with the world of other species, the sense we have that most arouses the feeling in us of being moved and touched." Here, behind these fences, I know that animals meet some of our needs.

<hr/>

In the spring, after the days have lengthened and temperatures have risen enough to drive cold-weather visitors like blackbirds away from the prison, a small, dirt-blond mammal starts poking its head above ground. Outside the perimeter fence, between the grassy "wetland" and a no-man's land of electronic sensors and scraped earth, the round-tailed ground squirrels have opened up their tunnels, pushing out winter's earthen plugs like mushroom hyphae throwing up fruiting heads. Prairie dogs, most of the guys call them, and, certainly, the squirrels do look like their grassland cousins. Both have the same light brown coloration, large, liquid black eyes, and cowrie-shell ears. Roundtails, however, are half the size of prairie dogs and have long slender tails (hence the name) as opposed to short stubby ones.

The squirrels have been hibernating since September, curled fetuses in underground, climate-secure wombs. Now they scamper in short bursts among tunnel mounds, dragging fat, dark bellies stuffed with seeds and the new leaves and flowers of dandelion. Flowers are a treat, especially those of the spiny ocotillo, whose blooms appear only where the landscape crews haven't tamed them by cropping their upper branches—some bizarre form of floral compliance to prison grooming policy, where even plants are emasculated and then displayed for visitors. During the foresummer drought of April and May, when dry, sterile winds reduce most plants to inedible tinder, the squirrels scale the wicked stems to get at the candy-red blossoms, the branches arching and swaying under the animals' weight.

Some of the roundtails are swollen with pregnancy. By summer, young roundtails will be climbing out of a dark, three-dimensional world to push the boundaries of this flat, sunlit landscape, even slipping through the fence to shoot down the runs and chase one another among the concrete tiers and flower beds of the housing units. It's these squirrels that some inmates look for; the young and inexperienced ones make the best pets. According to the men I know who have caught them, they're easier to train and adapt well to captivity. Byron had one in his cell for four years, a runt he raised from a litter of six. He caught the mother in a wire mesh trap he made in sheet metal shop, baiting it with a piece of apple. When the babies were weaned he released them but kept the smallest. "It had been rejected by its mother," he told me, "and I knew it wouldn't survive if I let it go."

It surprises me how successful the men have been with ground squirrels. I've always known the animals to be abnormally delicate, prone to disease and vehicle impacts. Unwary of hawks and coyotes, most won't survive their first season. It's as if they were born to be protein for predators, caviar for carnivores. Every year, my daughters try to "save" the little targets once their cats begin announcing spring by carrying them squealing into the house. But they've never had much luck. Regardless of their efforts with bottle-feeding and other forms of mothering, even uninjured squirrels end up cold and stiff within a week. Every time, they give me the same progress reports: Raincloud caught a baby squirrel; we're feeding it special food and it loves it; it's running around the cage and making a nest; it's hiding all the time and won't come out; it's not moving; it died last night. Then, the emotional trauma. I often wonder if my daughters would not be better off if the cats just ate the varmints.

Byron was a better mother than any of my daughters. His baby roundtail, a female he named "squeaky," thrived on a diet of apples, bananas, peanut butter, and almonds, living in a small cardboard box where it constructed a nest of shredded toilet paper. Byron soon had his pet "house trained" to use a newspaper-lined corner of his cell, as a kitten would use a litter box. He also trained it to come when called, the squirrel running up his pant leg to settle in a hand or on a shoulder. This allowed him to take his pet out for walks on the prison yard. "I usually carried her in my pocket," he explained to me. "But even when I put her down on the ground, she never went far and always responded to my whistle." Fortunately, most of the guards either didn't care or didn't know about the squirrel. But on one occasion, when an officer "shook down" Byron's cell intending to dispose of the squirrel, his pet seemed to sense something was wrong. It remained hidden until the guard gave up the search. I've heard about other inmates who train their pet squirrels to disappear quickly with the sound of a hand clap. The guards have never caught on to the real purpose behind the applause.

Byron cared for his ground squirrel for four years, until

Round-tailed Ground Squirrel

his classification changed and he became eligible for a lower custody facility. He knew the animal couldn't survive a return to the wild, and a bus trip across the state would be impossible. On the day before his transfer, Byron gave his pet to a man who promised to care for it as long as it lived. The man wasn't going anywhere; he was doing life.

I've read about the effect keeping pets has on prisoners. Some states allow inmates to have small animals—fish, caged birds, hamsters—in their cells, and studies have shown the result to be therapeutic. Caring for animals reduces stress and decreases behavioral problems. In an environment that generally promotes selfish behavior as a necessary skill for survival, pets are a contradiction. They demand attention. And more. They demand affection. In the simplest way, pets allow us to feel empathy toward something besides ourselves, another life outside our own, and they give us an opportunity to respond to that feeling in a real way. Byron was so attuned to his pet (which, in turn, recognized and accepted him by smell) that he noticed whenever the squirrel was too hot or too cold by the condition of its fur. He certainly sympathized with it, too. On those occasions when the animal climbed to his window ledge to stand on its hind legs and bark in frustration to some distant and unseen presence, Byron could relate to his furry companion. He knew no answer would come.

The other day, six men carried a kitten across the prison yard to the classrooms. Five men huddled around one man with a kitten as if it were a Christmas food package from his mother. It took half a dozen men to make sure the kitten would get into the hands of a teacher where they believed it would be safe, where it would find a home.

I often see cats in this prison. They stalk the yards after lockdown, abandoned pets and strays that turn wild and secretive, untouchable, living on mice and birds and handouts. The men buy cans of tuna from the commissary for them, leaving the food out at night and only rarely seeing what eats it. In this way the men adopt the feral cats. The kitten brought to the classrooms, a black long-hair with soft gray eyes, was different from its estranged relatives here. It was affectionate. Some inmate had tamed it. It spent the day wandering around the desks, chasing wrappers, and sleeping in a box under the computers. The students handled it every moment; it got all of our attention. When someone made a ball of yarn for it, its play occupied us as much as it occupied the kitten. Before it went home with the prison psychologist, I allowed myself to pet it. I knew better but ignored the warnings. As it nosed my palm and purred, my own unexpected emotion caught me. I choked, swallowed hard, and hoped no one had noticed.

Some emotions are the underside of life in prison. A hidden part, because inmates see them as weakness. They are always there, just below the surface, those unacceptable feelings of sorrow, of pain and fear, but we must not express them. Skin, the body's perimeter fence, must be tough, impenetrable. It's the code. Only anger and hatred are allowed. In the same way that the prison environment deprives us of touch, we, in turn, deprive ourselves of being wholly human. It is a common reaction to doing time—easy time, it's called. But it's also a coward's way of dealing with prison. In my mind, turning away from emotion, and the reasons behind the emotion, is what is weak. Many people hide in prison. Its very nature isolates and insulates; it constructs barriers deeper than walls and fences. It makes it easy to slip inside your own comfortable and private cocoon. Easy time. No remorse, no depression, no pain. It's weak. It takes courage to face the pain, to expose yourself to the consequences of your actions and accept them, particularly the consequences that affect your victims, your family, your children. I could allow myself to pet the kitten because I'd already accepted that I'm going to do hard time. I touched it and became vulnerable, but it wasn't weakness. The kitten connected me to my three daughters who, at that moment, had three kittens of their own. But they didn't have me.

Catclaw Acacia

March 18, 1997
High 86°F Low 54°F
Clear

Five-thirty AM. The yard opens in a half hour for breakfast. My cell mate sleeps under his woolen blanket. I see it, frozen in the predawn blackness, from across the cell where I sit in a chair. Comet Hale-Bopp. The narrow window in the steel door frames it perfectly, as if it were a painting by Kim Poor. It is a star smudge; its tail drifts opposite the unrisen sun like a finger pointing to the future.

There have been too many comets in my life. Too many blurred fingers directed at me. Last March, when I was on my way back to prison, Comet Hyakutake marked my northern sky. I watched it on the nights of its closest approach to earth as it swung toward perihelion, and I felt its significance. Hyakutake should have meant nothing to me. It was a rather minor clump of ice and dust in an elliptical orbit around the sun. Nothing more. I didn't think I believed in the evil portents and disasters ("bad stars") linked to these visitors. I enjoyed amateur astronomy. Astrology was for the superstitious minds.

When Comet Shoemaker-Levi made the news in 1994, I watched the reports on television from my cell. For the first time in history, scientists would record a collision between celestial objects as Jupiter swept the dirty slushball from its orbit like a vacuum sucking up a dust mote. That same summer, important events were also taking place in my own life. A judge had agreed to hear my petition for post-conviction relief. There was the possibility he would reduce my sentence, even release me. When my wife surprised me with this news in visitation, I lifted her off her feet and spun her around. But after one full turn my legs became tangled and we both crashed solidly to the ground. I should have known then, even without the comet's message, that any freedom would be doomed.

As I write this, I remember another comet in my life, this one more ominous. My final year as a teacher ended with my crime. I had chosen a path that would lead to a twelve-year prison sentence, probably the least of its devastating consequences. The summer of 1986. Only a few months before, Halley's Comet had brightened the night sky for the first time in seventy-six years.

When dawn comes, Hale-Bopp fades in the east. This morning, seeing the apparition centered in my window, I suppose I should wonder whether a change is coming for me. But I don't. I don't wonder at all.

The man wearing eyeliner sits on the toilet to pee.

What are you doing? I think.

"I don't mind if you stay," he says. "I'm used to it."

"I'll leave," I say.

"You don't have to. At Cimarron you wouldn't have a choice. They keep us locked up twenty-three hours a day."

I go outside. On the run, men are coming back from work for the noon lockdown and count. It's Tuesday, movement day, and there are unfamiliar faces. I hate losing a good cell mate.

The toilet flushes and I go back in. "I'm Ken," I say.

"I'm Mark, but I like to be called Marra."

I pause, look at him. His hair is long and stringy. He's balding. Like me, he wears a blue chambray shirt and denim jeans. Prison blues. "Hi, Mark," I say.

When the yard opens again after count he starts having visitors. Men I've known for years who wouldn't normally speak to me come sniffing around like dogs. Now we're instant friends by association. Mark greets them all with a smooth barstool voice. "What's your name?" he asks. He softens to strangers at the door and makes easy conversation that hints of availability, vulnerability. I'm embarrassed. I wonder if he knows what he's doing. The men laugh at him. But they stay.

Evening now. Lockdown. The run is quiet. A guard moves from cell to cell, looking into windows, making count. Mark unpacks boxes. He places his shirts on hangers, top button buttoned. On a shelf his pants lie folded. Next to them are his white boxer shorts and tube socks. He doesn't wear socks. From one box he pulls out a sweatshirt, which is navy blue and oversized, triple X.

"I had to pay someone to get this for me," he says.

I look up from my book. "What for?"

He slips it over his head and the sweatshirt hangs, mid-thigh. "I like the way it looks on me," he says, and rubs his hands down his front.

I go back to reading Terry Tempest Williams's *An Unspoken Hunger*. She writes: "Hands on the earth, I closed my eyes and remembered where the source of my power lies. My connection to the natural world is my connection to self—erotic, mysterious, and whole."

"I guess you know by now I'm gay," Mark says. "Bisexual actually. I like women, too. I was married once."

I watch him twist his thin hair into a braid at the nape of his neck. He has delicate fingers.

"It doesn't bother you, does it? That I'm gay, I mean."

"No," I lie. And then use a convict line: "As long as you respect me, I'll respect you."

The next day I stay away from my cell. I walk extra laps on the exercise track watching for birds. I sit in the inmate park and write in my journal. My thirty-five-cent-an-hour job as a teacher's aide in the afternoons becomes a retreat. But I'm bothered by thoughts of what might be going on back at my cell. *My house.* I have a reputation. I'm straight, moral, and I don't want anyone thinking otherwise. Particularly in this place.

After work another face I've never seen before peers into my cell. Mark's not home. I open the door and a young black kid tells me he's got something for Marra. He hands me a soft bundle wrapped in a brown paper sack and asks me to give it to her. Later, Mark slips a white cotton bra from the sack and holds it up to me.

"Can you believe it?" he says, excitedly.

I can't. Where did someone get women's clothing in a man's prison? I think he must have sewn it himself.

Mark wants to know if his friend can get him panties as well. He can, for a price.

Traffic increases through the late afternoon to the evening lockdown. Some men want Mark to braid their hair. Others just want to talk. An older Mexican national at the end of the run has been trying to hold Mark's hand. Mark thinks it's cute. "You sure can tell there's a new queen on the yard," he says, referring to himself.

Before the yard closes, Mark shaves his body in the shower. Now, he tells me he loves the way a new razor makes his skin feel, his arms, legs, chest. While I read, he preens in our novel-sized mirror and complains he can't shave all of his back. He waits for me to respond. I say nothing. I concentrate on my book. Williams writes: "Our lack of intimacy with each other is in direct proportion to our lack of intimacy with the land. We have taken our love inside and abandoned the wild."

Mark carries the mirror, a lamp, and his hobby-craft box over and sits beside me at our desk. He uses a black China marker as eyeliner, first heating its waxy tip with a Scripto lighter and then tracing the margins of both upper and lower eyelids. When he shows me the result, I think: *Egyptian princess.*

"Do you paint?" I ask, after he lifts a set of watercolors from the box.

"Not the way you think," he says. He mixes a burgundy shade on a well-used part of the palette and applies it to his lips with a fine brush. The color is too dark, unnatural. It accentuates the thinness of his mouth and his pasty skin. "What do you think?" he asks, looking straight at me. He has no expression, but there's tragedy in his eyes.

"Too much," I say.

Mark wipes his lips and tries again. This time the color is grape Kool-Aid. "That's better," he says. "I'll wear this tomorrow. Maybe the guards won't notice."

When I get home from work the following day two guards are searching my cell. They want my colored pencils. Mark gives them his China markers instead. "I can get more," he tells me later.

I'm upset about the shakedown. Mark draws attention from guards as well as inmates. It all makes me nervous. I'm a private person, and I enjoy what little solitude I can get in this place. "I'm gone most of the day," I explain to him finally. "In the evenings I'd like a little peace. No visitors. No underwear salesmen." I don't say any more, but I start hoping Mark will move out soon.

After dinner we have fewer guests, mostly men who live on my run. One in particular is persistent; I see him the most. He's young, maybe twenty-five, and has a lankness that's developed into poor posture. His accent is corn-fed Midwestern; my stepfather would call him a stupid hayseed. The kid's presence in my cell, a space only seven by twelve, makes my follicles squirm. He's playing the prison game, trying to earn acceptance from the white racists—the recent, half-finished tattoos that march up his skinny arms give it away. Political ink. Now, he massages Mark's shoulders and back. He's desperate for the status he will have for owning a "fem." At least he wants people to think he's after status. He's asked to be Mark's "man."

"I'm not interested in another relationship," Mark volunteers later that evening after the kid is gone. "I just had a man at Cimarron, and I'm not ready for that yet. My people here will see that I'm protected."

Cimarron is the Tucson complex's high security unit. A lockdown facility. Gang violence is a way of life there, a place, Mark tells me, where there are only two kinds of inmates: predators and prey. I wonder what it has cost him for protection. Gangs sometimes brand people they own, a warning of property rights to rival groups. Human property rights. Homosexuals. Sex slaves.

Mark has brands, so he calls them. His are self-inflicted, narrow bracelet and anklet burns he made with a heated, straightened paperclip. "I don't scar easily," he says, and points out places on his arms and shoulders where other white blazes have begun to fade.

"Why do you do that to yourself?" I ask. Yesterday, Mark showed me an angry infection where he had pierced the flesh of his navel. He claimed it didn't hurt and, over my objections, proved it by pushing the entire length of a straight pin under the skin of his forearm. He had already punched a new hole in his earlobe with a green push pin.

But the brands and scars have nothing to do with ornamental ear and navel rings. "Why?" he says. "Because I know how to get what I want. It's in my file. The cops know if they mess with me I'll cut myself."

Mark looks at me, fish-eyed and emotionless. He's in the back of his mind somewhere. I remember his concern that I might wake up in the night to his screams.

I say nothing.

"See these," he says, touching a string of white puckers like the beads of a rosary draped across his arm. "They are my atonements."

"I know of a better atonement." It's the only thing I can think of to say.

"I know what you're going to say. I know you're a Christian. It won't work for me. There's no forgiveness for what I've done."

Mark had killed his wife. He had told me already. He said he was doing ten years for manslaughter, but he didn't offer any details and I didn't ask. In prison, it's disrespectful to ask about another man's crime. He'll tell you about it when and if he wants to. Real convicts don't pry into another man's affairs.

"That night we had been drinking and doing drugs," he says. "There was a noise outside; the dog was barking. I guess I was paranoid from the cocaine and was thinking someone was trying to break in. I thought it might be the cops. I kept a Chinese SKS assault rifle and had a Berretta 9mm next to the bed. I grabbed the rifle and headed for the door. She tried to stop me. The gun went off."

Mark's eyes glaze again, and he's expressionless. But I know there is pain behind the blankness. "You got ten years for an accident?" I say, cautiously.

"They thought I murdered my wife. They said I fled the scene. I don't remember everything that happened afterward …" Mark pauses. "Parts are missing, but I know I tried to call the police from a pay phone, then drove across the border into Nevada and turned myself in. I was soaked with her blood."

Mark slides a box out from under the shelves. "I have pictures," he says. "They wouldn't let me keep them all, the gruesome ones, but I have these." He lifts a large stack of color prints held together with a fat rubber band.

"You don't have to show me," I say. "I'm not sure I want to see them."

He says: "They're not bad," and sets them one at a time in front of me. "I got them from the investigation. I'm appealing my case."

The photographs are dark, glossy. Many show blood stains—smears on a door, footprints and track marks on the floor, spatters on the ceiling. There are several of the weapon, empty beer cans, the inside of a stainless steel sink.

"Those are pieces of bone in the sink," Mark says, pointing out several white polygons like pieces of eggshell. "The top of her head was blown off. The autopsy report said the bullet entered just above the left eye and exited the upper back of her skull. She died instantly. I have a copy of the autopsy. Do you want to read it?"

I'm shocked by his clinical objectivity. "Mark, how do you deal with this?" I have trouble imagining the horrible mistake, its horrible consequences. There's more than one victim here.

A week later I'm noticing queens. The Santa Rita Unit has four separate yards, and on my yard alone there are at least five of them—*fems*. Three whites, a Mexican, a black. The other yards have them, too. Mark knows some of them from

Cimarron Unit and other facilities. They hang out together like birds, walk the yard in coveys of four or five, and flirt with passersby. I see them everywhere.

One afternoon, a young Hispanic "girl" sits at the end of my bunk to visit with my cell mate. I read; they chat about hair and makeup, relationships, P.M.S. It's hard for me not to get drawn into their conversation, and I do at various points, but mostly I feel like excusing myself and leaving them to what Mark calls their "girl talk." Lately, Mark has grown interested in someone.

"I'm sure you two will make a nice couple," says Patty. I don't know his real name. His hair is long and black and drawn into a ponytail high on the back of his head, an obvious feminine touch.

"I promised myself I wouldn't get involved with anyone again, not right away at least. But I really like him," says Mark.

"I think it's great," says Patty.

"We need to find someone for you. What about that cute Mexican chick who moved in upstairs?"

I think Mark is making a joke, but I'm not sure. This conversation has cornered me. I want to leave but don't want to embarrass myself by getting up now for no apparent reason. Instead, I pretend to ignore them.

"God, Marra," Patty says. "I'm *not* a lesbian."

The statement surprises me. In my mind I unwind it until it makes sense: A man who believes he's a woman thinks he will be a lesbian if he's attracted to another man who believes he's a woman.

That night we eat saltines and oysters that Mark has bought from the commissary. He stacks the smoked mollusks, drip-

ping with oil, on the square crackers and hands them to me
one at a time.

"This is becoming a habit," I say, taking each offering
from his deft fingers. "Oysters, sardines, kipper snacks—I'm
eating all your food."

"I always take good care of my cellies," he says.

"You do ..." I say, and then stop, realizing the implica-
tions of his words. Mark often plays with innuendo as a way
of testing the water. Roman bath water. To him, people are
simple. You are either homosexual or homophobic.

"My people want me to move down to yard three," he
says. "I told them I'd think about it; I'm happy here."

"Is that what you really want?" I ask.

"I know you think they just want to use me. But they are
my friends."

We've talked about this before. That time it concerned
another recent arrival who was beaten and chased into protective segregation because "she" had betrayed these same
"friends." They said she did favors for nonwhites, what Mark
calls being a race traitor.

"They only want one thing," I say.

"Sex," he says.

I look at him. Neither of us says anything. I can smell his
perfume, and it's sickly sweet, omnipresent, and cheap—the
kind ugly women wear to bars.

"You know there are people here who will be your friend
without ... that." I want to add "like me" but the words don't
come. I'm hesitant about the commitment, still fearful of
what people might think, or of something else. Mark inter-
feres with my need to keep a low profile.

Mark doesn't agree with what I said, however. "They are
the same," he says. "Sex and friendship. It's what everyone

wants. It's what I want too. All my life every friendship has been sexual, since I was eight, when my older brother began abusing me. Every relationship I've ever had involved sex, lots of sex. My wife and I were swingers, did I tell you that? I've had dozens of women, and more men. Sex in prison is how I survive."

That night I wait for sleep to come and think about Mark's words. Above me, in his bunk, he snores softly, like a woman.

I understand survival in this place, and it concerns me, too. I survive by finding distraction in books, by teaching and writing, by connecting with the nature I encounter here. I escape into barn swallows and Sonoran desert toads, into pollen-spiced insects foraging in desert willow. This is my passion. It's all I know how to do.

Terry Tempest Williams: "If we ignore our connection to the land and disregard and deny our relationship to the Pansexual nature of earth, we will render ourselves impotent as a species. No passion—no hope of survival."

I also understand atonement. I, too, seek atonement for my past—only my seeking is a long string of repetitive, unanswered prayers. My own rosary in the flesh.

A month after he moved in, Mark is gone. On Friday, when I return for the noon lockdown, I have another cell mate. The change is so complete, so smooth and painless, that for a few minutes I don't realize what's happened. I'm used to visitors, unfamiliar faces in my house. Then, suddenly, I'm disappointed. Mark is with his people now, with the kind of friends I was unwilling to be. His new cell mate, I'm certain, will call him by his name, by her name.

Desert Willow

Gambel Oak

THE IMPORTANCE OF TREES

On every lap during my exercise walks I pass the length of the prison visitation park. Although the metronome rhythm of my steps and thoughts may distract me elsewhere, my eyes always turn to the trees. I have a bond with them; they are familiar friends. They, like other bits of wildness confined or visiting here, expound some vital part of me in the midst of prison's two heavy hands: fear and depression. In the same way they break down the stark gray walls and cut holes in the fences, these trees particularly lessen the burden of this place. I don't know what kind they are—Chinese elm sounds nice—but they are dark and hard-green, thick with promise, though they have no more years than my oldest daughter, a teenager. I do know that these trees do not come from the desert. They are too deciduous. They are trees in need of wells.

With all the activity among the tables and trees in the inmate park, the chess games, cards, reading, guitar playing, the quiet contemplation, I wonder why we no longer have access to the visitation park. No one uses it anymore. A cage encloses the covered tables, barbecues, and grass, its gates padlocked against unlawful entry. (TRESPASSERS WILL BE PROSECUTED: an irony almost as acute as the "keep off the grass" signs that pop up here every so often.) When the park was accessible years ago, I probed its grassy regions for toads and bugs with my daughters, grilled boneless chicken breasts on Sunday afternoons, picked heady roses for my wife. But picnicking inmates quickly fell into disfavor with the public. I guess we behaved too much like real families gathering together after church. Security was a problem, so we were told (security is a blanket that covers all reason), and the park was closed. A simplistic solution from an administration with all the imagination of a lock and key.

Since then my girls and I have walked small circles—a kind of perpetual motion in prison and always in a counter-clockwise direction—in the concrete visitation area, with its people-crowded ramada and tables and sandbox, hoping that the climate will change and the tree-shadowed grass of the park will become more than a cruel tease, a flagrant reminder of how much worse things can get.

Things do get worse.

This evening, burnished clouds of sunset darken to the color of unfermented wine and the moon is as pale and thin as a communion wafer. The Santa Rita Mountains in the south are flat and undefined, a purple matte framing a sheet-metal sky.

All day the landscape crews have been at work in the visitation park. They began by sledge-hammering and digging out the picnic tables and grills. They moved on to the trees when the backhoe arrived. At first I thought they might try to save these, to relocate them, perhaps at the farm. I even imagined they were using the chainsaw to prune the trees somewhat, making them easier to handle. But this was my own fantasy; the tables and grills and flowerbeds and trees are all coming out. It's finally over for the visitation park. No more cruel tease. No more trees.

I admit I'm irrational about it. It's only a dozen trees and I'm calling it a clear-cut. I want to do an Ed Abbey on the backhoe. I'm harboring a secret wish (wrongly) that the officer in charge of dismembering the trees will lop off his own arm with the chainsaw. I'm angry, helpless. I think it is a decision made in spite. I walk past a picket line of obscene treeless trunks and see muscular arms with chopped-off hands reaching upward in some kind of plea for the maimed and dying. I'm irrational because I value something here. I've risked love. My emotional response is the evidence. These trees did more than dissolve the gray walls and dull the razor wire, rebreathing and purifying the very cast of this prison. They were more than an analgesic to numb my punishment, the fear and depression. They were a kind of living point of reference that gave me a sense of direction—physically, yes, but more so emotionally. The trees helped me to keep my bearings on how I felt about my family. Because we had shared them together, and because they hinted of rope swings and summer climbs, of names carved in wet cambium, they were firmly rooted metaphors of the love I have for my daughters, my wife. The trees connected me to a reality beyond prison.

I guess I shouldn't be angry. I shouldn't expect everyone to value the same things I do. Not in this world. There are people who willfully separate and distance themselves from nature as if they could exist independent of wildness. It is a kind of disobedience, the same kind that separated us from

God in the beginning. I try to practice a faith that teaches that God gave us dominion over the earth, but somehow, I think, we've misunderstood this gift, its purpose. Perhaps our definition of dominion has changed as we've distanced ourselves from both God and nature. Perhaps we never understood the word. Nature writer Michael Katakis was right on point when he wrote: "We took the idea of dominion over the world and its creatures to mean ownership rather than stewardship and then raised ourselves to a place we had not earned and we're not suited for. We do not do well as gods." We, in fact, were never supposed to be gods. We were supposed to be gardeners. As gods, we tend to lean toward destruction rather than creation, cutting down and rooting up rather than cultivating.

My eyes still turn to the trees. It's a habit I prefer. What I see in the visitation park, however, is more gray, more buildings, fences, razor wire. The trees are gone now; there's a barrenness that seems unnatural, and it leaves an emotional hole in me like the one I feel each time my wife and daughters exit these gates after visiting me. More obscenity: earthen craters pock the ground in the place of tree wells; torn vestiges of rootstock twist skyward in the place of trees.

I don't expect I'll ever again see that gray flycatcher in the park. I know the western kingbirds will never rebuild their nest. I won't sit in the shade with my girls and chew on grass stems they offer me or watch them roust toads or pick flowers—not here anyway. Those are family things not intended for this place.

Things change. The visitation park stands empty in a cage.

New Mexican Locust

March. In the inmate park a few white iris blooms peel open in hopeless rebellion. They are alone. The rumor started by the chainsaw wielding guard that the inmate park was next is no longer rumor. The park has been a problem for some time. The peppertrees have grown too tall. Someone could climb one, hide among the branches, and imagine he's escaped. Or someone could lie down and disappear into the roses and mint. (Someone might even be brewing illegal tea from mint leaves!) Crews with the chainsaw and backhoe work feverishly to correct the error in security: all the rose-bushes, privets, the Texas ranger, all the Mexican bird of paradise, the desert willow—they're coming out, cut down, chopped into sections, wrenched from the ground. The few peppertrees that survive the clearing can't take much more pruning. They lack all lower branches, their skinny trunks winding comically into high, tight crowns like trees in a Dr. Seuss story.

The policy of tree-cutting spreads its infection to the yards. Already concrete has capped off the flowerbeds in front of all the runs, entombing flower bulbs and toads, and the landscape crews have torn out the ocotillo, barrel cacti, and agave. Now it's the yucca, the catclaw acacia, the New Mexican locust in front of my cell. Shrubs are the greatest risk to security; they all go. And more trees....

It bothers me that I had to come back to Santa Rita to witness this trend in Arizona corrections where trees have become superfluous, shrubs and flowers a threat. In two months the unit will go to controlled movement. No more open yard. The inmate park will close. The track will close. Even now a fence rises on the edge of the soccer field, soon to be our exercise cage for outside recreation at scheduled times. When that happens we'll have Bermuda grass. The park will lose its purpose. The trees their meaning, except to the chainsaws and backhoes.

I try to console myself by remembering that I will be gone in a few months. The classification board has reduced my public risk score and has recommended another unit, minimum custody. After more than eight years here, I have to leave Santa Rita. Maybe it's time. A minimum unit should allow me the freedom to explore another wilderness behind fences.

I still believe there will always be some wilderness here. An untamed remnant that slips inside. Without trees and flowers and weeds there will be less diversity: fewer butterflies, fewer beetles, fewer bats and birds. Others will adjust, however.

There will always be ravens.

Creosote Bush

Rumors of barn swallows have preceded some unusual weather. A storm approached southern Arizona yesterday, heaving up a horizon as greasy and black as a skillet. It was charged, twin fronts of energy exchanging glancing blows and splitting the air with their violence, scattering ravens, if not swallows. I could smell it coming, and it was the smell of summer. But the storm never closed the distance, never got past being a scent, a little moisture steeped with creosote and escaping on the wind.

When I came back to prison seven months ago I encountered another storm and fell into its violence. While I dragged my bag of sheets and blankets across Meadows Unit they watched me. Even their eyes kicked me with thick-soled boots. I discovered polyps of inhumanity among the guards, too. I was vulnerable because I hadn't much skill at keeping lies. Prison isn't a place where you can wear disguises for long. In prison, you wear your face as it is. In almost nine years now, I've met all kinds. I know a man who can't help exposing himself in public. He sleeps sucking his thumb. There's another with a third grade education who washes people's laundry as a favor so he won't be forced off the yard. He was abused as a child. Now, he's abused as an adult. Another, this one not yet out of his teens, sings the same monotone songline over and over each evening behind the chow hall. A lonely old man, his only friend, watches him for hours in the darkness. And then there's the queen who's concerned about missing his period. He believes he might be pregnant.

For most people, prisons tend to be things over there, those places we look at from the highway but don't go near. We catch a scent of their edges and wonder about their centers, their insides. They are for many of us places of secrets we don't care to uncover, to learn about, regions of brooding darkness on the horizon best left to itself.

Ignorance has no conscience, no emotional baggage. It leaves hardly a slick on the surface of the mind.

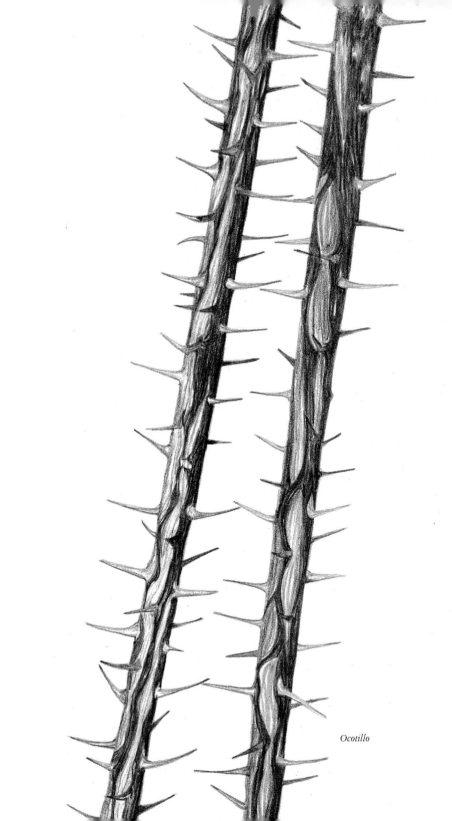

Ocotillo

On the way back to my cell after work I tuck my head and hands into my sweatshirt and pull my arms across my chest. I step quickly, my senses narrowed down to a margin of ground directly in front of me. My mind focuses on getting out of the wind and nothing else until something distracts me. A disturbance of blackbirds. Two are fighting, tumbling as one bird on the dead Bermuda grass. Two dozen more draw a donut barrier, chattering wildly as if they were school children egging on rival playground bullies. My presence scatters most of the crowd, and in the lull I see that one combatant has pinned the other. It's not a blackbird; there's a black stripe across its eyes. It's a shrike.

I move closer and the shrike cocks its head at me. Instantly, the blackbird flushes, but the predator pursues and takes it at the perimeter fence. I watch the shrike with the blackbird and forget about the wind and dust. Other men move past me on their way to their cells; everyone feels the effect of the changes. I just stand there, a stalled vehicle at an intersection. As friends approach I point to the scene but have few words, and most of these are jumbled, nonsensical. "Did you see that?" I ask, and they look at the birds and back at me. "It's a shrike! It's nothing nice. Killed it. Chased it to the fence." My enthusiasm mystifies them. *So what?* their faces say.

———◦———

I don't believe that nature only occurs in "wilderness." I also don't believe that wilderness, by definition, has to be uninhabited. Wilderness is not always the land absent of people; but the land absent of human control.

I said in the beginning that my wilderness is a prison. Maybe this seems a leap in rational thinking. We think of wilderness as a place that covers remote and vast terrain where humans lack influence and the land cycles according to its own rhythms—migrations and monsoons. The place must be wild, unexploited. We say that wilderness should have predators, large carnivores like mountain lions and grizzly bears that link us to the food chain, placing us on an intimate level with deer and cottontail rabbits. This is ideal wilderness and it hardly exists.

My wilderness has some of these elements. It isn't vast (yet at thirty acres or so, it fits within the category of some of our designated wildernesses of less than one hundred acres), but it is remote. It's outside the city. My wilderness isn't autonomous—prison is all about control—but, to the degree that fences, razor wire, and security systems can't control the weather, the seasons, or even the birds, insects, and seeds that drift in, wilderness asserts itself. Certainly, my wilderness is diminished—much of it is pruned and mowed, hoed, sprayed, and penned—but not everything. Here, a summer thunderstorm is my wilderness, the runelike shapes of swallows, a chorus of oblate toads. My wilderness is a logger-

head shrike taking down a blackbird, a red-tailed hawk feast-
ing on a raven, a horned owl watching for mice outside my
cell. Although no large predators reside here to remind me of
my tenuous place in nature—unless I consider the human
kind—plenty of small predators inhabit this place. My wilderness is weeds and coyotes that persist along the perimeter
fence, bugs and bats and rodents that ignore it. My wilderness is every uncontrolled, impenitent bit of nature that vio-
lates the rules of this place.

Indeed, prison as a wilderness is a leap in rational
thought. But here, for me, wilderness is a state of mind as
much as it is a place or even an experience. I don't need weeks
alone in a vast tract of uninhabited space to rid my mind of
worldly concerns and tune my body to the rhythms of wildness. I haven't distanced myself that far; I haven't been human—civilized—that long. Like every other living thing,
I am still made of earth. I share organic molecules with fungi.
I get hungry, thirsty. I desire companionship. I respond to the
circadian and seasonal ebb and flow of chemicals in my
blood. Wilderness exists because I am aware of it.

I hear quite often from other inmates that I don't have a
prison sense, that I'm not aware of what really goes on
around me. They refer to the dark underside of prison: the
racism, homosexuality, extortion, manipulation, and gangs.
The staff tells me this too. Several years ago when doctors di-
agnosed Jessica with Juvenile Rheumatoid Arthritis after she
unexpectedly contracted into a ball of fragile bone and muscle, some inmates attempted to send my family money to
help buy her a wheelchair. When the prison administration
discovered this gesture, an assistant to the warden threatened
to lock me up in protective isolation—not a pleasant way to

do time. He said I was naive to allow inmates to put me in this position, that I would now "owe" them and my life could be in danger. The truth is, despite my naiveté, I never was in danger. The administrator was perpetuating an absurd myth that all inmates are alike, that we are all incurably criminally minded and are always looking for opportunities to prove it. "An inmate is an inmate is an inmate" he is fond of repeating, his personal mantra and message. I've learned differently. I've found compassion among the men here. I know the under-side of prison exists. I've seen the brutality of it—the brutal acts of guards as well as inmates. Both are susceptible to the infectious sadistic disease this place harbors. Confinement breeds its own base behaviors, those like targeting certain inmates—snitches and sex offenders—for the group's ag-gression. Animal behaviorists call this "scapegoating" and see it clearly in caged animals kept in overcrowded conditions. I see it every day. But what I should be accused of is ignoring it, not ignorance of it. I choose another awareness, one that centers on the preservation of my spirit. The other only leads to fear and paranoia. I need only enough of this kind of prison sense to keep me out of the "games," to keep me out of trouble. Anything more is a fixation, irrational, self-destructive. I prefer a prison sense that stirs me to the wistful cry of a new species of bird or the discovery of a new wild-flower. I'm thrilled to see Orion swinging overhead in win-ter's darkness.

In *Songbirds, Truffles, and Wolves* Gary Nabhan writes: "If you cannot find terrain magnificent enough to take your breath away, gravitate to places that can at least increase your heartbeat … It needs to be land that allows the possibility of glimpsing wolves, untamed truffles, and unexpected migrant birds, land where you sense their presence in your pulse, land where their fragrance catches and lingers on the breeze."

For me, it is this place, where coyotes, toadstools, and migrating swallows ignite my senses, pump my blood, and sometimes even leave me breathless. Wilderness, I've decided, *is* a state of mind, an attitude, and a deeply personal experience. I can share its elements with others, but the experience of wilderness, how these elements touch me, comes from a place within me that I don't fully understand. It's a place entrenched with relics of childhood and family, this I know for sure. My wilderness absorbs me, so much so that time, like pain, can't be remembered. In this, wilderness is a kind of salvation. It helps me to live day to day, to be mindful of the choices that brought me here, but also to continually push beyond the memory of those choices, my choices, to make something better of my life … to heal others, to heal myself.

There is wilderness here. It rubs against my life.

By evening the wind has settled and I can walk laps without collecting a layer of dust under my contact lenses. April will be the last month for the track, as our perimeter is slated to shrink significantly beginning in May. Controlled movement means walking in smaller circles only when we're told, but we will walk. I'm thinking about this and hoping I'll soon be on a minimum yard but still near my family—nothing is certain in prison except the fear of uncertainty—when something dark and agile shoots past my face, too agile to be a sparrow or blackbird. I snap my head to the right and watch pointed wings rise slightly and then dip over the razor wire. It's a profile I haven't seen since October. They're back! Another season has passed and the swallows have returned!

Century Plant

A NEED FOR MOUNTAINS

Sometimes what seems like surrender isn't surrender at all. It's about what's going on in our hearts. About seeing clearly the way life is and accepting it and being true to it, whatever the pain, because the pain of not being true to it is far, far greater.

—Nicholas Evans, *The Horse Whisperer*

From this bunk, my window allows me to look at the Santa Rita Mountains on the southern horizon. The view hasn't changed much, only the window—it opens.

I write these words nearly six months after my transfer from the Santa Rita Unit. The months have not been easy. It is a new year now, 1998, just into my tenth year of incarceration, my thirty-ninth year of life. Last summer I came to Echo Unit, a facility of military tents and industrial trailers that houses more than four hundred men at the Tucson complex. Finally, minimum custody. Echo is an open yard. Unlike Santa Rita now, this unit allows the men to move about freely, to go to work and meals and recreation unescorted. Echo is a place of grass and trees, sidewalks and park benches; there's an exercise track that traces the perimeter. Here, old men sit with doves on their shoulders. I think of it as a monastery more than a prison. A good place to do time. At Echo, rimmed by familiar mountains, I can walk laps, watch birds, visit with my family.

For two months after my arrival, I settled in as a tent dweller, working again as a teacher's aide, playing guitar in church. I continued with the creative writing workshop, traveling back to Santa Rita on Saturday mornings. I also got to enjoy home cooking again. At my first food visit, a quarterly privilege for minimum custody prisoners only, my wife and daughters brought shish kebabs, a fresh summer fruit salad, and cherry pie. It was a picnic, and we all got sunburned. The next food visit, we learned, would fall on my birthday in November, a surprise my girls were more excited about than I was.

Then something unexpected happened.

On September 25th, as hurricane Nora traveled northward across the Gulf of California toward Yuma, Arizona, Echo Unit went on lockdown. Another storm was gathering in the desert and rushing in Yuma's direction: one of the largest mass movements of prisoners in Arizona history—all sex offenders, hundreds of them, from all over the state. But I couldn't have known that at the time. When two officers entered my tent and told me to roll up, I didn't believe them. It had to be a mistake; I wasn't supposed to go anywhere.

The sergeant I questioned thought I might cause a disturbance—my first indication of the magnitude of the move. What he wouldn't tell me was that the department had reclassified me and many others as predators because a new state law had been passed.

It came with the stroke of a pen. Retroactive with the U.S. Supreme Court's marginal approval of a similar law, whereby sex offenders could be held in custody beyond their release dates for an indeterminate length of time, Arizona's sexual predator law came into effect. One of its stipulations: sex offenders will now be considered violent, even first-time offenders previously classified as nondangerous and non-repetitive. Now, the Arizona Department of Corrections had a problem. There were inmates whose custody status no longer applied housed in less secure, minimum institutions. These could be committed to mental hospitals once their sentences expired. Suddenly, there were hundreds of security risks in prison across the state.

At Complex Intake and Processing the cages bulged with men. Officers on extra duty tagged our property with yellow tape—Yuma, I had been told. Then, in leg shackles and belly chains, we boarded the buses and left Tucson. All I could think about as I stared through a heavily screened window at the receding mountains was how far away Yuma was from my wife and children. Four hour's distance might as well have been three year's.

Because of the storm we spent the night at the Perryville facility outside of Phoenix. It wouldn't be the first night I attempted to sleep in a lockdown cell on the floor. In the morning we drove south toward Gila Bend and the interstate, passing volcanic plains, creosote flats, and sand. More and more sand. The Yuma prison complex, I learned, isn't in Yuma but settled into the sand dunes three miles from the Mexican border.

Later Friday afternoon, I was part of the last wave to arrive at the Cheyenne Unit, a medium custody, controlled movement yard. The prison looked familiar. It was a clone of Meadows Unit—the separate yards (north and south) and dormitories, the administration area, even the intake cages. Cheyenne's similarity to Meadows disturbed me. I didn't want a repeat of what happened to me there last year.

We paced inside the cages for hours waiting for housing assignments. Dinner came in paper sacks, bologna on white bread and sickly sweet orange drink. After dark the temperature began to drop. What was taking so long? We were anxious and uncomfortable. I still hadn't shaken the irrational feeling from the afternoon that we were being bused into the sand dunes for execution. When several men suddenly jumped up and scattered away from one side of my cage, and the largest scorpion I'd ever seen—longer than my boot— crawled under the chain link, I couldn't ignore the message. Welcome to Yuma prison.

Then something happened on the north yard. Officers appeared from the administration building and ran across the tarmac, their radio's squealing. IMS. Inmate Management Systems—an incident in process. Within minutes, the officers had men in custody. A bandage covered the side of one's face. Another man they locked into the last empty cage, leaving his hands cuffed behind his back. He watched us for a while in the dankness and then said, "We know who you are."

We didn't get our housing assignments until after midnight. Four men refused them, choosing instead to take disciplinary reports and go to lockdown. During the evening, details about the earlier movement waves of sex offenders trickled into the cages. Yuma inmates were confronting new arrivals about the nature of their crimes, asking for paperwork. Those who couldn't produce it, or wouldn't, were being assaulted and beaten in the shower, in their bunks, in the chow hall. Cheyenne wasn't supposed to be a "political" yard. Officers said it would be safe for us. The gangs were here, however. The unit had gone on indefinite lockdown; the warden had restricted all activity, doubling, then tripling security. But the added presence of brown shirts walking the runs only compounded the problem for us.

Reluctantly, I took my assignment and dragged my bag of bedding onto the yard. I was the only one sent to Pod 10-c, and it disturbed me to be separated from the group. At Meadows Unit I had been alone. It wasn't so much the fear of discovery, the rejection. I'd been dealing with rejection for years—the stares, the furtive words and gestures, people leaving when I sat down at the their table, others spitting on the ground when I walked past them. It wasn't even the overt threats. What worried me wasn't the inmates. I didn't want the department consigning me to protective custody far from my family for the remainder of my sentence.

I didn't last twenty-four hours on the Cheyenne yard. It *was* Meadows all over again, only this time I knew what to expect and was prepared to defend myself against injury. When inmate threats against me led to staff threats—"If you won't tell us who's involved, we'll send you back to the dorm"—I refused to comply, even when the assistant deputy warden explained my disobedience would increase my risk score as a sexual predator. But I was among company. Men from Echo had already been hurt. Lawyers were making calls. Dozens of us went to the hole rather than stay on the yard. Investigative lockdown. For the next two weeks my eyes pulled in a view through the narrow slot of thick glass. My horizon was undefined except by an ebb tide of sand, and I began to believe that sand and the sky could trade places without notice.

The department eventually realized housing sex offenders at Cheyenne had failed. Men who were not hospitalized began escaping the yard to the already overcrowded Central Detention Unit. Local media reports only catalyzed more unrest among the inmates. Something needed to be done. It took three buses and a caravan of trucks and vans pulling trailers to transport more than a hundred men and their property. It was a parade. Officers in chase vehicles stopped traffic at intersections along our route to the interstate. Television crews, newspaper reporters, and sightseers stationed themselves at the roadside outside the prison. All were witnessing the exodus from the desert. The predators were leaving Yuma.

Cook Unit, a deputy warden had told us, and I knew the place. I had seen it more than a year before. It's part of the new Eyman complex at Florence, the same prison complex where Meadows is located. Meadows, in fact, sits right beside Cook. But I didn't get past the sally port entrance before several officers culled me from the group. My attorneys, working with my wife, had discovered a mistake that raised my classification level. Upon my return to prison, the department had classified me as a repeat offender. Despite court documents that said otherwise, my release had been in error and I had committed another crime, according to the computer. When a captain of security pulled me from a line-up of inmates, unshackled me, and put me in a van headed for Tucson, I cried. I was the only one to come back to Echo.

➤─┤◆➤─0─◄◆├─◄

In today's paper, a candidate for Arizona's attorney general hopes to win the election with a new tough-on-crime stance. He wants the death penalty for sex offenders.

Nothing is certain. I used to have peace here, despite the place, but it escapes me now. Anxiety comes with every rumor of movement, and the rumors have substance. It could happen again, at any time. My number appears on the screen, a body out of place, a need for "population adjustment" due to a new law. Two months after my return to Echo it happened again. An officer ordered me to roll up; I was being transferred to Florence, to Cook Unit. I knew it was a mistake, the same mistake. I made a desperate call home. Then, I explained the situation to every officer who would listen— guards, sergeants, counselors. No one would try to verify my information. The computer said I had to go. In the end, after getting a disciplinary write-up for disobeying a direct order (I went to work instead of reporting to the vehicle gate for transfer), a sympathetic officer finally checked on my status. He canceled my move as I was loading my property onto the bus. I had stalled long enough for my attorneys to correct the problem. At the phones back on the yard several hours later, I noticed an administrator watching me. "You have a yo-yo string on your back," she said.

"Who can stand in the presence of mountains and remain unchanged," asks Hal Borland. In *Fear Falls Away*, Tucsonan Janice Bowers writes about visiting the limitless "oppressiveness" of central Montana and coming to realize her need for mountains: "Never before had I understood how badly I need limits to my horizons." After my unexpected trip to Yuma, I, too, discovered a need for mountains on my horizons. It was more than missing mornings sipping coffee in sight of Sentinel Peak, west of Tucson, knowing my wife was waking to her day only a half mile away from there.

More than missing a familiar skyline, the sloping shoulders of the Catalinas, the rising hips of the Rincons—an absence I felt as acutely as I felt the absence of my sleeping wife next to me in bed. I missed the mountains' deeper significance. I came to prison because of a lack of boundaries in my life, personal boundaries. But it wasn't the fences that corrected me. I have stood in the presence of mountains … and I know I am a different person. They remind me I've changed, that I have found healing.

As I approach the end of my sentence, I think more and more about what horizons my life will possess without all this razor wire. I will never teach again—I couldn't do that to my wife—and Karen has had enough of law and politics, of prison, of Arizona. It's a shame, a tragedy really. I love this state, its drive-by desert and sky islands, those regions beyond the fences. I wasn't born here, but Wendell Berry says being native simply means knowing where one is. I know where I am. I have become a part of this place.

I expect that Karen and I and our children will leave Arizona. We'll find another state, or another country. We'll become expatriates. We'll find another wilderness. One we can really learn to call home.

KEN LAMBERTON

Raised and educated in the desert Southwest, KEN LAMBER-
TON graduated from the University of Arizona in 1980 with
a bachelor's degree in biology. He began writing shortly after
his incarceration in 1987, and since then has published more
than one hundred articles and essays about nature in magazines such as *Bird Watcher's Digest, New Mexico Wildlife, Tucson
Lifestyle,* and *Sport Literate.* Essays from *Wilderness and Razor
Wire* have appeared in *Snowy Egret, Northern Lights, Manoa,
American Nature Writing 1999,* and *The Gettysburg Review,*
among others. He is a former nonfiction editor of the *Sonora
Review* and is presently completing his M.F.A. in creative writing at the University of Arizona. He is due for release from
prison in September 2000.

RICHARD SHELTON

is the author of nine books of poetry, five chapbooks, and the recent award-winning nonfiction *Going Back to Bisbee* (University of Arizona Press, 1993). His poems and prose pieces have been published in more than two hundred magazines and journals, translated into Spanish, French, Swedish, Polish, and Japanese, and set to music by established American composers. Since 1974, Shelton has taught writers' workshops in the Arizona prisons. Eight books of poetry and prose by men in these workshops have been published, including the anthology *Do Not Go Gentle.* A resident of southern Arizona since 1956, he is a Regents Professor in the English Department at the University of Arizona.